# MASTERING

# EXECUTIVE

# PRESENCE

## Career-Advancing Communication and Presentation Skills

sienna

PUBLISHING

www.siennapub.com

ISBN: 978-1-7324155-0-8

Printed in the United States of America

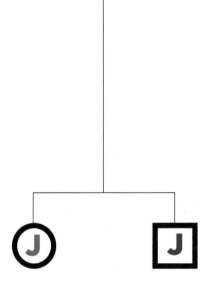

## ABOUT THE COVER

We borrowed from the genogram or family tree to delineate our
sibling authors. John is represented by the male square; Jenn, the female circle.
You'll see one symbol or the other at the start of each chapter so you'll
always know which author's point of view is prominent in each section
of the book. That said, the research and writing of every chapter was truly a
collaborative effort.

"*Mastering Executive Presence* is an extremely practical book – you will want to keep it readily available for reference and validation on how you are presenting yourself. The exercises and reflection tool are outstanding and sure to have an impact on readers' professional and personal lives."

*– Dennis McGurer, executive coach Upsurge Advisors*

"Writer and savvy social science observer Malcolm Gladwell said it takes 10,000 hours to achieve mastery in a given activity. *Mastering Executive Presence* is a terrific, two-hour read that will easily shave 500 hours off that 10,000."

*– Bruce Hennes, CEO & crisis management specialist*
*Hennes Communications*

"I can't wait to use this book to develop our Bobcat students. Executive presence – mastered early and practiced often with a wide range of audiences – goes a long way in extending an individual's leadership impact. We are honored to be certified to use the Vautier methodology to develop top talent business college students into next generation leaders."

*– Tim L. Reynolds, executive director Robert D. Walter Center*
*for Strategic Leadership, Ohio University*

"The content is superb, and I'm sure it will be the 'go to' source for media and presentation training."

*– Thomas A. Chizmadia, SVP-government affairs and communications*
*Lehigh Hanson, Inc.*

"*Mastering Executive Presence* is an essential read for the serious executive. The Vautiers provide real world guidance for those just starting their career, as well as for seasoned executives who want to stay at the top of their game."

*– Jim Nash, managing partner,*
*Marcus Thomas LLC*

## ACKNOWLEDGEMENTS

We are grateful to so many for their generous sharing of experiences, wisdom and talents. While many expert sources are acknowledged in the Notes section of the book, other friends, clients and colleagues who contributed significantly to the making of *Mastering Executive Presence* are not.

We wish to recognize ... **Chuck Bogosta** for his wisdom, candor and instructive stories from the C-suite ... **Tom Chizmadia** for his brilliant insights into the media and his valuable tips for exhibiting grace under pressure ... **Denny McGurer** for his inspiring ideas and enthusiasm around leadership, networking and communication ... **Erin Miller** for her marvelous observations and valuable lessons from the field ... **Tim Reynolds** for his incredible passion, practicality and optimism (lucky students!) ... **Matt Wey** for his trusted counsel and magnanimous support of the project ... **Rachael Haas** for her painstaking attention to detail in proofreading the manuscript ... **Ken Kesegich** for his thoughtful and insightful editing assistance ... **Laura Seidel** for her exquisite design and production expertise ... **Beth Hallisy** for her extraordinary writing assistance and project management skills ... **Kit Vautier** for her critical eye, voice of reason and good humor ... and **John Vautier, Sr**. for his energy, guidance and invaluable creative contributions throughout the project.

Thank you. Our book would not have been possible without you.

To our parents and lifelong coaches, John and Kit Vautier

# CONTENTS

## FOREWARD

I am excited to write this foreword for *Mastering Executive Presence: Career-Advancing Communication and Presentation Skills,* as the book speaks to my interest, which is helping people achieve success in their personal and business lives.

A person's success is generally founded on his or her relationships – that is, how well the person is regarded, respected, and trusted. Relationships in business, as in life, matter greatly. The better our relationships, the more effective we will be in achieving our goals. We don't do it alone so it's important people believe in us and want to work with us. Executive presence and strong communication skills allow us to achieve this end.

Authors Jenn and John Vautier offer sound, easy-to-follow advice about speaking with others – whether you're giving a speech, presenting to a group of high level executives, or engaging in individual conversation with a client or colleague.

Some of our conversations are one-on-one, some with multiple people, and some with large groups. They all matter. Each of us wants to be received as a knowledgeable and dedicated person who can be trusted. We want people to want to believe in us, to follow us.

Leadership, like relationships, happens one conversation at a time.

While nearly everyone would be well-advised to read this book, it's a must-read for people working in business – senior executives, mid-level high performers, and up-and-comers alike. Whatever our field, we all are in a people business, and how we show up means more than most of us realize. The wisdom in this book will help all who follow it. In fact, I wish *Mastering Executive Presence* was required reading for college students, as I believe it would help students interview better and gain the opportunities they seek following graduation.

So many great tips fill *Mastering Executive Presence*. I found myself nodding in agreement, underlining passages, making notes in the margins, and, very importantly, mentally committing to practice what I was learning. Simply, it makes sense!

I feel very strongly that reading this book will help each of us, no matter our age or experience. We all want to strive for improvement. I am eager to give copies of *Mastering Executive Presence* to family members, friends, and clients, as I know the book will help them be even more successful in their business and personal lives.

- John P. Keyser,
President, Common Sense Leadership, and author
of *When Leadership Improves, Everyone Wins*

## VAUTIER COMMUNICATIONS: THE NEXT GENERATION

Jenn and John – my children, business colleagues and two of the best executive presence coaches I know – have been communicating since before they were born.

Yes, I did say before they were born.

That's not tall talk or even parental brag-speak (which I admit, I can be guilty of). It's scientific fact.

In 2011, a couple of researchers in Italy proved that twins start communicating with each other in the womb as early as the 14th week of gestation[1] – which is pretty mind-blowing, especially to a parent of twins and a guy who's been in the communications industry for more than three decades. (I still wonder what they said about me in those early days.)

Scientists call this early, private language of twins cryptophasia – "crypto" meaning secret and "phasia" meaning speech. They also call it idioglossia when describing the language alone and not the accompanying mirrored gestures common with twins.

All I know is this incredible duo came out of my wife Kit's considerably over-stretched belly on October 31, 1987 – Jenn at 3:35 p.m. and John at 3:36 p.m. – communicating. And, seemingly, very effectively.

Quick story:

We're about six months into the parenting thing. Kit and I are still mesmerized by the twins and their twin-speak. One evening, we were having dinner in the kitchen. John and Jenn had been fed and were in the playpen in the family room, just down the hallway but out of sight of us. (On the advice of our pediatrician, we had gotten the XL playpen so the twins could be together and provide a certain comfort level to each other.) Maybe 10 minutes into dinner, we saw a toy float into the kitchen. Then another. And another.

This went on for a bit but we knew if John and Jenn saw us before we were done eating, they would want to be with us. And we had discovered early on that we couldn't eat too well holding on to two squiggling bundles, joys that they were.

So we finish dinner and then walk out to the family room to discover the twins had launched all their toys out of the playpen. More than that, in this very short period of time, they also had taken all their clothes off, down to their diapers, and lobbed every shirt, skirt, pair of pants, and sock over and out of the playpen. In my mind, there was just no way they could have accomplished this feat without a good deal of cooperation and superior communications skills.

But that wasn't enough for our twin disruptors. They not only wanted to get our attention, they wanted to change our behavior. Somehow the two of them masterminded a way to wiggle the XL floor pad out from under them, muscle it up over their heads and heave it a good few yards from the playpen. From that evening on, John and Jenn had us within eyesight. And from that evening on, we knew they'd grow up to be communications coaches.

OK, that last line may be a stretch. Our money was probably on discus throwers back then. But it did seem natural and right when they both, separately, decided on communications coaching careers.

Now you know a little something about Jenn and John, the writers of this book – which, by the way, is a sequel of sorts to *Speak As Well As You Think*, a book John and I wrote in 2013. That first book focused on helping readers gain confidence in their ability to communicate effectively and thereby elevate their executive presence. A lot has changed in our world, and in how we communicate, since then. But, of course, many communications tenets are the same. Oftentimes, we simply need reminders, relatable examples and practice.

In this much more interactive book, Jenn and John blend their own experience (and mine) with current, global best practices; introduce our proven methodology; share true stories from our clients, as well as other communications and business thought leaders; provide practical tools and tips; and offer opportunities for reflection and practice.

John and Jenn attempted to design the book in a way that would feel personal for each reader. The book encourages your participation. But you decide where to go, how long to spend there and when to come back. I have no doubt active readers will emerge more confident, more effective communicators.

Indulge me another minute or two? I think you'll appreciate this post-toddler-years insight into your coaches.

Here it is: They are sick competitors (and by sick, I mean what we used to mean when we'd say great or awesome, but with some fierceness on top). Jenn and John really enjoy one-upping each other. They like winning. They continuously challenge themselves to do better and always put themselves in positions to help others achieve whatever it is they want to achieve.

It's been fascinating and gratifying to watch John and Jenn throughout their lives gravitate back to each other – as study partners, lifeguards, swimming coaches and CrossFit® trainers. After college, John initially pursued an exciting sales and training career in the southwest U.S. with Whirlpool. Jenn was called to a career in education. So each has been coaching, teaching or training in some form or another for more than a decade.

Judging from client feedback and an unheard of 88% repeat engagement record, they excel at what they do. Just as importantly, they love it. They are truly inspired by the commitment and the positive change they see in the people they coach. They know the work they do has impact. Every single time.

Each reader of this book, and every professional we coach, brings his or her own set of circumstances and his or her own personal growth goals to the experience. But whether you're just beginning your career or you're a seasoned pro, you will benefit from the read. You will advance your goals.

Achieving executive presence is a lot like achieving the ideal fitness level. It's a lifetime commitment. The work never really ends. But there is real joy and great satisfaction from the many wins along the way. As you most likely already know, it's well worth the effort.

Enjoy the read. Make it personal. Come back to it when you need a reminder, a fresh idea, a little nudge, or inspiration to knock the next one out of the playpen. Er, ballpark.


My best,

John M. Vautier, aka John Sr.

# ACHIEVING YOUR PERSONAL BEST

J

"We convince by
our presence."

– WALT WHITMAN

I'm constantly playing back advice a friend gave me in college:

**"Bite off more than you can chew, and then chew it."**[1]

I thrive on challenges. I love to get outside my comfort zone.
That's when I feel most energized and motivated.
That's how I learn and experience positive change.
I expect the readers of this book are much the same.
You wouldn't be investing the time, otherwise.

So, let's get after it!

## A WORKING DEFINITION OF EXECUTIVE PRESENCE

In short, when we talk about executive presence, we're talking about the
ability to demonstrate a certain ease, confidence and effectiveness when
communicating. Several years ago, a *Harvard Business Review* article described
executive presence as "highly intuitive and difficult to pin down" but it
"ultimately boils down to your ability to project mature self-confidence ...
take control of difficult, unpredictable situations ... make tough decisions in a
timely way and hold your own with other talented and strong-willed members
of the executive team."[2]

In her book *Executive Presence*, Sylvia Ann Hewlett says "it's an amalgam of qualities that telegraphs that you are in charge or deserve to be ... It's a measure of image ... (a) signal to others that you have what it takes, that you're star material."[3]

Hewlett devotes a chapter to "gravitas," which she maintains is a key component of executive presence. "Gravitas is the very essence of executive presence," she says. "Without it you won't be perceived as a leader, no matter what your title or level of authority, no matter how well you dress or speak ... (It's) what signals to the world you're made of the right stuff and can be entrusted with serious responsibility."[4]

The top six aspects of gravitas, based on research Hewlett conducted with senior leaders, are

**1** confidence or "grace under fire,"

**2** decisiveness and "showing teeth,"

**3** integrity and "speaking truth to power,"

**4** emotional intelligence,

**5** reputation and standing or "pedigree,"

**6** vision and charisma.[5]

**More advice from**
***Harvard Business Review:***

"Look for opportunities to hone your presentation skills. Not only is public speaking an important executive requirement, but your ability to "stand and deliver" to an executive group or large audience is frequently viewed as an indicator of your ability to handle pressure. Rehearse major presentations until you can come off as relaxed and in command, and pay special attention to the Q&A portion since your poise when questioned and ability to think on your feet help you project a sense of self-confidence.

Most important, find your voice as an executive: that is, identify your assets and leverage them to the hilt. Some people are naturally gregarious and can fill a room with their personality. Others ... rely on their listening ability, sense of timing, and ability to maintain their composure when others get emotional. In an increasingly diverse world, executive presence will look very different from one executive to another. However, the constant is building the confidence of others that you can step up as a leader when times get tough"[6]

We don't coach people on gravitas, per se; we believe it's something that comes largely from within and is earned over years of doing the right thing. But Hewlett suggests steps we can take to get us on a path toward gravitas. We all would do well to incorporate these into our personal and professional repertoires:

- **Surround yourself with people who are better (smarter) than you.**

- **Be generous with credit. Shine a light on others.**

- **Stick to what you know.**

- **Show humility.**

- **Smile more.**

- **Empower others' presence to build your own.**

- **Snatch victory from the jaws of defeat (when given the opportunity).**

- **Drive change rather than be changed.[7]**

## HOW COACHABLE ARE YOU?

When researching and writing this book, we had a particular type of person in mind. Perhaps surprisingly, we didn't focus on age, gender, title, tenure, industry, public speaking experience or communications competence. When defining who would benefit most from this book, we thought more about the personality characteristics and behaviors of people who excel in our programs and one-on-one coaching sessions. It's not important to us if you're a managing partner, a physician, a computer programmer, a student, a CFO or a lemonade stand operator. We see the most extraordinary results when we work with people who are self-aware, have a desire to learn, are open to change, and are willing to work.

One of my favorite pieces on coachability was written for *Forbes* by August Turak, who was, among other things, a founding member of MTV. He maintains that authentic change requires humility, an action bias, purity of purpose, a willingness to journey into uncertainty ("insisting on certainty is just another bogus constraint we impose to stay off the hook") and faith.

"The problem with life is that it must be lived forward and only understood backwards," Turak explains. Often times, we don't realize how much more can be accomplished. He gives the example of an alcoholic who only understands the benefits of sobriety when he successfully changes his behavior.

"Usually things get worse before they get better," Turak says. "Only hindsight is 20/20, and that is why we so often hear someone exclaim, 'If I knew then what I know now I would've changed years ago.'"[8]

**Getting to and maintaining a high level of executive presence starts with a clear vision and the courage to evolve.**

## IT'S READY, SET, THEN GO

When the people we coach have goals and can articulate specific outcomes they'd like to see from our work together, we – not surprisingly – dramatically increase the likelihood of our achieving those outcomes together.

What do you want to accomplish, be it in your personal life or your career? You have to be able to name it. Sure, your goals may change. Yes, there likely will be detours and bumps in the road. But before you embark on anything – even a learning endeavor like reading this book – know what you want to gain from it. And share your goals with people who can help you achieve them.

Time for one of my favorite Yogi-isms: "If you don't know where you're going, you'll end up someplace else." There has to be intent.

About five years ago, I got talked into signing up for a triathlon that was taking place four weeks later. I figured I was in good enough shape. I was regularly running and doing CrossFit®. How hard could it be? I wasn't trying to win the thing. I did the bare minimum and, while I finished, it wasn't pretty. It's never very satisfying to simply finish when you know you could have done much better. Not to mention, I put myself at risk of being hurt. As soon as registration opened for the following year's event, I signed up. For that one, I had an end goal and milestones to reach along the way. I did my homework, stuck to a training schedule and naturally performed much better. Preparation not only delivers better results, it makes life a whole lot easier, too.

People very rarely become better tennis players, chess players, pianists, dancers or chefs without conscientious practice. The same is true for adept communicators. If we want to be truly effective, if we want to be among the best at what we do, very deliberate practice is a must. And not two days before a big presentation.

One of the best illustrations I can think of is the practice range at a PGA or LPGA tournament. You often see the pros hitting the same shot repeatedly, seemingly with great ease, precise form and amazing accuracy. Yet, they repeat the shot dozens more times. Similarly, on the putting green and in the bunkers, players practice seemingly flawless shots, over and over again – even after having just finished playing 18 or 36 holes. That's why they get to be a member of such an elite group.

As Vince Lombardi said, "Practice doesn't make perfect. Perfect practice makes perfect." Any good coach will tell you they'll take 10 perfect reps over 100 inconsistent ones.

## WANT TO SEE CHANGE? PUT IN THE TIME.

**The thing that distinguishes one performer from another is how hard he or she works. That's it. And what's more, the people at the very top don't work just harder or even much harder than anyone else. They work much, much harder."**

– Malcolm Gladwell,
*Outliers: The Story of Success*

The Gladwell quote above is in reference to a study of pianists and violinists at the Berlin Academy of Music. Studies also have looked at the performance of ice skaters, fiction writers, basketball players, even criminals. Interestingly, Gladwell shares that "researchers have settled on what they believe is the magic number (of practice hours) for true expertise: 10,000."

But don't hurt yourself trying to get in those hours too quickly. Gladwell also points to studies that suggest true mastery typically requires at least a decade.[9] (To save you the math, you'd need to set aside about three hours per day for 10 years to get to that 10,000-hour sweet spot.) While natural talent, encouraging environments, the right tools and knowledge play a part in our ability to perform,

there is no getting around the fact that purposeful practice – and lots of it –
is what really moves the needle. Executive presence requires practice.
I'm sure you saw that coming. We're coaches; when has a coach not encouraged
practice?

While 10,000 hours of practice is the prescribed investment of time to achieve
mastery in a given activity, imagine how much better you'd perform if you simply
practiced 10 hours before an important meeting or 20 hours before a significant
speaking opportunity. More is better. But any amount of practice will improve
your game. Assume a direct and positive correlation between the number of
hours you invest and the results you experience. Then it's your call how much
time you want to invest. We'll provide more tips on practicing later in the book.

## REFLECTION: WHAT'S YOUR OBJECTIVE?

Before reading further, we encourage you to think about and write down
– in very specific and measurable terms – what you want to gain from
reading this book, and what kind of time you want to devote to improving
your communication effectiveness.

**How** and **why** do you want to change as a speaker, presenter or
communicator? Imagine having just made an important presentation to
a prospective client, given a talk to new employees or delivered a speech
at an industry conference. What do you want your audience to be thinking
and saying about you afterward?

# EXERCISE: KNOW WHERE YOU ARE AND WHERE YOU'RE GOING

## A Self-Assessment and Visualization Exercise

Below are several word pairs. The words in each pair aren't meant to be polar opposites in meaning. Nor is one word in the pair negative and the other positive. That said, most of us probably would like to fall closer to the right side of each continuum when presenting. Take several minutes to think about your last few presentations – be they to a large group, small group or an individual. How would you rate yourself? What would your audience say? Circle a number on each continuum. Then, go back through the word pairs, and decide where you'd like to be in a specific amount of time. Circle those numbers. Then highlight the space between the two circles for each set of words. Where are the largest gaps? Think about how you can close these gaps as you continue through this book.

| Nervous | | | | | | | | | Confident |
|---|---|---|---|---|---|---|---|---|---|
| 1 | 2 | 3 | (4) | 5 | 6 | 7 | 8 | 9 | 10 |

| Distracted | | | | | | | | | Comfortable |
|---|---|---|---|---|---|---|---|---|---|
| 1 | 2 | 3 | 4 | 5 | (6) | 7 | 8 | 9 | 10 |

| Hesitant | | | | | | | | | Focused |
|---|---|---|---|---|---|---|---|---|---|
| 1 | 2 | 3 | 4 | 5 | 6 | 7 | (8) | 9 | 10 |

| Confident | | | | | | | | | Gracious |
|---|---|---|---|---|---|---|---|---|---|
| 1 | 2 | 3 | 4 | 5 | (6) | 7 | 8 | 9 | 10 |

| Fidgety | | | | | | | | | At Ease |
|---|---|---|---|---|---|---|---|---|---|
| 1 | 2 | 3 | 4 | (5) | 6 | 7 | 8 | 9 | 10 |

| Aloof | | | | | | | | | Expressive |
|---|---|---|---|---|---|---|---|---|---|
| 1 | 2 | 3 | 4 | 5 | 6 | 7 | (8) | 9 | 10 |

| Robotic | | | | | | | | | Poised |
|---|---|---|---|---|---|---|---|---|---|
| 1 | 2 | 3 | 4 | (5) | 6 | 7 | 8 | 9 | 10 |

| Guarded | | | | | | | | | Approachable |
|---|---|---|---|---|---|---|---|---|---|
| 1 | 2 | 3 | 4 | 5 | 6 | (7) | 8 | 9 | 10 |

| Reserved | | | | | | | | | Enthusiastic |
|---|---|---|---|---|---|---|---|---|---|
| 1 | 2 | 3 | (4) | 5 | 6 | 7 | 8 | 9 | 10 |

| Cool | | | | | | | | | Warm |
|---|---|---|---|---|---|---|---|---|---|
| 1 | 2 | 3 | 4 | 5 | (6) | 7 | 8 | 9 | 10 |

| Unpracticed | | | | | | | | | Expert |
|---|---|---|---|---|---|---|---|---|---|
| 1 | 2 | 3 | 4 | 5 | (6) | 7 | 8 | 9 | 10 |

What change are you committed to making? Revisit this page in one month, six months or a year. And then periodically after that. We think you'll be pleasantly surprised at the incremental progress you will make simply by focusing on optimal behaviors and practicing.

## THE LASTING FIRST IMPRESSION

02

"I knew when
I met you an
adventure was going
to happen."

— A.A. MILNE

The thing about first impressions:

**They last. They last as long as forever.**

Research study after research study has borne this out.
An impression you make in seconds can literally last a lifetime.[1]

For a first impression to change, it has to be challenged in multiple different contexts, concludes Bertram Gawronski, the lead researcher in one such international study. "But, as long as a first impression is challenged only within the same context, you can do whatever you want," says Gawronski. "A first impression will dominate regardless of how often it is contradicted by new experiences."[2]

A little daunting, isn't it? But there's no denying it: We all make decisions about people in an instant. Our experience tells us our snap judgments are accurate the vast majority of the time. So we trust them, and won't easily let them go.

## THAT MAGIC MOMENT

I started my career in teaching, and I can tell you first impressions in the classroom matter big-time. And they last. Students can be brutally unforgiving if they don't like and trust you at the outset. But if they do trust you, the connection can be powerful. Tremendous learning and growth can take place.

I'm sure you have a favorite teacher or perhaps a coach. Think about an early encounter with that person. How did he or she make you feel? Please take a minute here. Are you smiling? Are you feeling inspired, motivated?

In his wonderful *Little Book of Talent*, Daniel Coyle makes the point that "good teachers use the first few seconds to connect on an emotional level." This helps them earn that essential trust quickly. Making those early connections with students was game-changing for me.

And when I think of my two favorite coaches – my high school basketball coach and, of course, my dad – I will tell you, they made me feel 1) very special and 2) like I could do anything. I knew from the start they had my best interests at heart, and I could trust them. Together, we could push the limits. That feeling doesn't go away easily.

Coyle points to "lots of tools for making this early emotional connection – eye contact, body language, empathy and humor being some of the most effective," but he says above all else, "before you can teach, you have to show you care." Too often, we think we have to distance ourselves from people or rise above them to be effective leaders. Nothing could be further from the truth. Want to get someone's attention and respect? Show you care. (Coyle's chapter "Six Ways to Be a Better Teacher or Coach" was based on in-depth interviews with master coaches, and is well worth reading. We'll revisit Coyle's *Little Book* later. )

For now, we want to focus on that moment when you walk on stage, enter a classroom, greet your new team, meet a prospective employer, sit down at a boardroom table to present six months' worth of research ...

## How do you want to be perceived?

While coming across as confident is a good thing, appearing arrogant is not. There can be a fine line between the two. Our advice always: Give yourself every opportunity to make positive first impressions. Changing a first impression is just tough, tough sledding.

 **The sophisticate is a man who thinks he can swim better than he can and sometimes drowns himself."**

– Oscar Hammerstein

**When are you at your best?**

**REFLECTION:**

Think about a time when you were at your best, when you felt energized and effective. What did it look like? How did you get there? Remember the feeling when you make your next entrance.

## AND THEN IT HAPPENS

Fair or unfair. Right or wrong. People will make decisions that will greatly affect your life, literally, in the blink of an eye.

In his bestselling book *Blink*, Malcolm Gladwell references a study of married couples by psychologist John Gottman. Incredibly, Gottman could analyze an hour of a husband and wife talking and predict, with 95% accuracy, which couples would still be married 15 years later. If he observed the conversations for just 15 minutes, his success rate only dropped five percentage points. More astounding, when non-experts viewed 15-minute videotaped conversations with married couples, they also could predict which marriages would survive, with 80% accuracy, and which marriages were going to end in divorce.[3]

Gottman and Gladwell make the point that we all are very good at "thin-slicing," at sizing up complex situations very quickly and coming to "snap decisions." In the military, extraordinary generals are said to have "coup d'oeil," or the "power of the glance."[4]

Sure, it's possible to dig yourself out of a hole. People do give second chances. But wouldn't you much rather start off on level ground, or even high on a hill?

 **The task of making sense of ourselves and our behavior requires that we acknowledge there can be as much value in the blink of an eye as in months of rational analysis."**

– Malcolm Gladwell, *Blink*

## WE'RE IN THIS TOGETHER

As communications coaches, we strive to deliver immediate tangible results to our clients. Or why would anyone come back for more? Very few people like the idea of getting in front of a room and speaking, let alone being videotaped and critiqued. It's terrifying for some people and uncomfortable for most. Especially in group settings.

Our goal is to facilitate an esprit de corps where people feel supported, energized, and motivated to learn and experiment with new behaviors. So making a positive first impression is critically important for us. No one wants to be coached by someone they don't like or trust.

Over the years, we've learned the single most important thing you can do to gain a person's trust is to simply be yourself. Be consistently, authentically you. All kinds of experts in all sorts of books conclude the same. No one likes a phony and most of us can spot one in a nanosecond.

"Also, people are happier and more satisfied and have better relationships and greater feelings of purpose when they believe they come across authentically," says Heidi Grant, Ph.D., a senior scientist at the NeuroLeadership Institute and associate director for the Motivation Science Center at Columbia University. "Life is simply easier and more rewarding when others 'get' you and provide you with the opportunities and support that are a good fit."[5]

**If only that were as simple as it sounds.**

I think we all agree that "being yourself" can sometimes be a little tricky. We have different selves for different situations. We are complex beings and we can't project every part of who we are all the time. And, unfortunately, we all have good days and bad days, filters and prejudices. We can think we are coming off one way and be perceived by our audience completely differently.

"You can't sit back and wait for those around you to accurately size you up," says Grant. "You need to think strategically about encouraging and incentivizing them to see you in the best possible light."[6]

**Let's think about this some more.**

Can you think of a time when you may have jumped to the wrong conclusion about a person?

Boy, can I! Let me quickly share two experiences that come to mind. They were definitely learning moments for me.

First, I remember early in my teaching career, I came dangerously close to making a judgment about a student I truly believe could have changed the course of both our lives. My too-quick impression of the young man, whom I'll call Jason, was made in large part due to unsolicited comments expressed by Jason's previous teachers. When Jason walked in the classroom with long hair, sloppy clothes, a big grin and an arsenal of wisecracks at the waiting, it would have been easy for me to assume the worst and shut him down. In truth, I almost did. Fortunately, something about Jason – his wit and his earnestness – helped me see through his bravado and see another person entirely. Jason's subsequent success in my class ignited a steady reversal of his academic trajectory. I can't claim he made the honor roll, but his attendance and grades improved significantly, enough to graduate, which no one would have predicted. That nearly doomed first encounter turned into a big win for both of us. The moral of the story: You can't judge a book by its cover. But people will.

So, we say: sweat the cover.

## A WORD ABOUT WARDROBE

Our advice when it comes to dress is to know your audience, and dress accordingly. As TED's content director, Kelly Stoetzel, says, "You'll probably want to dress somewhat like they do, but a little smarter."[7]

You definitely don't want to insult folks by dressing too casually, nor do you want to come off as superior by dressing too formally for the circumstances. Don't wear something new that you haven't yet tried out. Wardrobe malfunctions happen. Stick to the tried and true. And don't wear anything too big or loud or otherwise distracting. Stoetzel goes so far as to recommend rehearsing your talk in the outfit you plan to wear. That eliminates one potential last-minute stressor.

Here's a bit more advice from Stoetzel:

> In most settings, all that matters is that you wear something you feel great in ... You don't want the audience's first unconscious thought about you to be any of the following: stodgy, slovenly, tasteless, boring, or trying too hard ... Believe it or not, your clothing can earn you an audience connection before you've even spoken a word ...
>
> The audience loves bold, vibrant colors, and so does the camera. Fitted clothing tends to look better on stage than outfits that are loose and baggy ... Make sure it's the right size – not too slack, not too tight ...
>
> The most important thing is just to wear something that boosts your confidence.[8]

Sylvia Ann Hewlett has a little different view. She says, "Once you're over the (executive presence) bar, you can start playing with the dress code ... Win everyone's faith and confidence. Then make your own rules."[9] We concur this is generally the case, particularly in creative and tech industries.

I also can recall jumping to an incorrect first impression during a group coaching session. A few people came quite late and without apology to the session. One, in particular, was especially loud and disruptive when he entered the room. Let's call him Frank. Frank seemed to pay little attention to me or his colleagues. His focus was on his handheld device. I almost let him get the best of me. (Fortunately, I employed a little trick to win the day, which I'll tell you about later.)

In reading the evaluation Frank left, I discovered I'd made a mistake in assuming he was rude and arrogant and unreceptive to learning. It turns out that Frank thoroughly enjoyed and benefited from the program. He even went so far as to say our program should be mandatory in his company, and he provided a list of referrals. I discovered from his evaluation that he was taking notes on his handheld.

Note to self: Many people multi-task effectively. Lack of eye contact doesn't necessarily mean a person isn't actively listening. There are myriad good reasons for tardiness. I was hasty (but not unreasonable, given his behavior and body language).

If we want to present ourselves favorably, we're much better off dressing the part, being on time, assuming good posture, being attentive, making eye contact and so on. Why leave something so important to chance?

 **A gentle word, a kind look,
a good-natured smile can work wonders
and accomplish miracles."**

– William Hazlitt

## YES, BE YOU. BUT, BE THE MOST ENTHUSIASTICALLY PASSIONATE **YOU** POSSIBLE.

*The Wall Street Journal* columnist and former speechwriter Peggy Noonan knows how important authenticity is to persuasive communication. Some might question if a major network newscaster should sound folksy or if a U.S. president should use non-words and uncomfortable pauses when conveying serious news. But this insightful, award-winning speechwriter knows a thing or two about winning the hearts and minds of her intended audiences. Genuine language breaks down barriers and inspires. It wins every time.

# REFLECTION:

We're all familiar with the expression, "Fake it till you make it." Amy Cuddy, Harvard Business School professor, social psychologist and TED Talk rock star, is known for tweaking that expression. She says, "Fake it till you become it." What does "it" – the optimal you – look like?

## Who do you want to become?

"When I worked for (Dan) Rather I'd find myself saying, 'You look like you been rode hard and put to bed wet,' and 'He's got a lot of off-road miles on him.' When I worked for (President Ronald) Reagan, I found myself going, 'Well ...'"[9]

Amy Cuddy talks of an aha moment in her book *Presence*. A visiting student asked for some feedback on data she collected from 185 entrepreneurial pitches to potential investors. The strongest predictors of who got the money were confidence, comfort level and passionate enthusiasm. Those qualities came through primarily in nonverbal ways – things like posture, voice quality, inflection, gestures and facial expressions.[10]

I love this passage from Cuddy's book:

> Presence emerges when we feel personally powerful, which allows us to be acutely attuned to our most sincere selves. In this psychological state, we are able to maintain presence even in the very stressful situations that typically make us feel distracted and powerless. When we feel present, our speech, facial expressions, postures, and movements align.
>
> They synchronize and focus. And that internal convergence, that harmony, is palpable and resonant – because it's real. It's what makes us compelling. We are no longer fighting ourselves; we are being ourselves. Our search for presence isn't about finding charisma or extraversion or carefully managing the impression we're making on other people. It's about the honest, powerful connection that we create internally, with ourselves ...
>
> Presence is about the everyday. It's even, dare I say, ordinary. We can all do it; most of us just don't yet know how to summon that presence when it temporarily escapes us at life's most critical moments.[11]

**That's the good news.**

We all have it in us to be our best, most authentic, enthusiastic selves.
We all can earn the trust and confidence of our audience. Once more, science has proven that there are "psychological and physiological mechanics to this sort of transitory presence."[12]

And we can learn and adjust and practice these mechanics.
That's what our next chapters are about.

I'll leave you with my top seven **Be's** to making a good first impression.

# ① Be you. No one likes a phony.

**2.** Be nice. A no-brainer.

**3.** Be prepared. Know your audience, your room,
your objective, your material. Preparation breeds confidence.

**4.** Be early. Take as much control of the room and
situation as possible.

**5.** Be interested. Ask questions. Listen.

**6.** Be interesting. That goes back to preparation.

**7.** Be aware of how you're heard and seen.
Perception is reality.

# KNOW THY AUDIENCE

J

"I have found that
sometimes it helps to
pick out one person –
a real person you know,
or an imagined person –
and write to that one."

– JOHN STEINBECK

When we coach individuals or groups – in any industry, at any level –
we have two overriding objectives:

**1** Help our client get to
and maintain his or her own personal
brand of executive presence.

**2** Ensure our client knows
how to organize and tailor a
message or set of messages
for the intended audience.

"Know thy audience" is really our golden rule. Effective communication has to start there. Too often, we waste time and miss opportunities by not understanding who we're talking to and what's important to them.

Prior to presenting information – or communicating for any reason – take time to learn everything you possibly can about your intended audience, as well as the environment where your communication will take place. There is simply no excuse to skip this essential step when considering how easy it is to conduct an online search, make a few calls and scan social media.

Beyond basic demographics and psychographics, like age, academic degrees, geography, work experience, title, etc., an effective communicator will understand his audience's knowledge of the subject matter, expressed points of view on relevant topics and possible objections to the material being presented.

"Even the best of the best have to prepare," says Denny McGurer, partner and executive coach at Upsurge Advisors and long-time friend, mentor and client of Vautier Communications. Denny recalls observing a speaker once who spent time in the back of the room getting to know audience members prior to giving his remarks. "By the time he got up to the stage, he was one of them," Denny says. "Then, he made eye contact with and addressed questions to those people in the back of the room. He used his knowledge of them to personalize his presentation. It energized the whole room."

"People don't fall asleep during conversations, but they often do during presentations – and that's because many presentations don't feel conversational," points out Nancy Duarte in the *HBR Guide to Persuasive Presentations*. "Knowing your audience well helps you feel warmly toward the people in the room and take on a more conversational tone," she says. "Speak sincerely to your audience, and people will want to listen to your message and root for and contribute to the success of your idea."[1]

When communicating with an individual or small group, we recommend digging even deeper. Get to know communication preferences, pet projects and pet peeves, favorite hobbies and athletic teams, family details, recent travels ... anything and everything you can possibly learn. Try to connect with them on LinkedIn or in other professional groups in advance of your meeting.

Beyond that, take into account your audience's mindset and schedule for the day. Will you be talking to someone who just endured a full day of back-to-back meetings, will be rushing to catch a flight, is facing a week of layoffs, just lost a significant piece of business, or is celebrating his 50th birthday? The more you know, the more you can customize your message, and the more likely it will be received as you intend.

"Knowing people – really knowing them – makes it easier to influence them," says Duarte. "You engage in a conversation, exchange insights, tell stories. Usually both you and they change a bit in the process."[2]

Your audience will appreciate your efforts and you will undoubtedly be more confident and relaxed in presenting your ideas. It's a win-win. Another long-time client and friend, Chuck Bogosta, who is president of both UPMC International and UPMC Hillman Cancer Center, says he makes it a point to (at minimum) read the biographies of everyone he is scheduled to meet. Often Chuck's meetings are with high-level government and health industry officials from other countries.

"I always try to find something about them and their country I can talk to them about," Chuck says. He recalls entering contract negotiations with a client in Kazakhstan: "The meeting had the potential to be intense so after everyone sat down and introduced themselves, I congratulated the group on their recent Olympic medal win. Everyone immediately smiled and began talking about the country's long preparation for and history with the Olympics. It brought the temperature down."

So simple and yet potentially game-changing. The next time you present, consider writing down everything you know about your audience. Then, ask yourself, what else is discoverable? How can you learn more and how can you use this information to be more effective?

 **You have to respect your audience. Without them, you're essentially standing alone singing to yourself."**

– K.D. Lang

## EXERCISE: UNDERSTAND THE AUDIENCE

Consider creating a form for yourself to ensure you understand your audience prior to preparing your remarks. Our form includes a description of the audience; number of people in the audience; location; time of day; length of talk; AV needs; audience attitude toward speaker and topic (on a scale from supportive to skeptical); decision makers and their critical issues; key influencers and their critical issues; purpose/objective of meeting (inform, persuade, inspire); key messages and takeaways (what do you want the audience to know, do or believe?); how decision makers have been successfully informed, persuaded or inspired before; and how you will deliver (extemporaneous, notes, text, handouts, PowerPoint).

 **EXERCISE:** GO ONE STEP FURTHER: BORROW FROM MARKETING AND DRAW A PICTURE

Marketers employ a tool to capture audience insight. Called personas, they are composite sketches of a target audience. Oftentimes, they take the form of "day-in-the-life" snapshots so marketers can visualize their audiences, put themselves in their shoes, and better appeal to their wants and needs. According to the Content Marketing Institute, "Without personas, you may only guess what content your audience wants, which means you are more likely to revert to creating content around what you know best (your products and company) instead of around the information your audience is actively seeking."[3]

Building an effective persona takes data, time and thought. Content Marketing Institute's Jodi Harris suggests asking a series of questions about your audience, some of which are relevant for our purposes. For example:

- **How influential is she in the decision-making process? From where might pushback come?**

- **Who else might influence her decisions (internal and external)?**

- **How far along is she in her consideration process?**

- **What questions is she likely to ask to satisfy her criteria for making a decision?**

- **What obstacles might stand in her way as she looks to satisfy that criteria?**

- **How does she like to get information?**

- **Whose advice does she trust or seek most?**[4]

Get a good picture of your audience in your head, or perhaps even down on paper, before you deliver your next speech or present your next big idea.

04

"The following three statements about top executives are all true: They sleep on Egyptian cotton that quintuples the thread count of your jersey-knit blend. Spigots in their autos are more valuable than your entire sedan. And they travel more often than The Biebs on tour."

–NICOLE VARVITSIOTES,
THE MUSE

Sometimes it can feel like there's a vast divide between you and the suits upstairs in the corner offices. Approaching seasoned executives in top positions can be unnerving. Our clients' and bosses' bosses can be complex individuals. They are likely wicked smart. They have many, many years of diverse experience. They also have enormous responsibilities and are under intense pressure to perform and to not do anything that could cost them – and their constituents – dearly.

**But they also are likely to be receptive to new ideas, open to change and willing to take risks.**

So, yes, communicating in and around top layers of organizations can be intimidating, even for seasoned executives. But CEOs want and need good input. They invited you in for a reason. They do not want you to fail. In fact, they are hoping and trusting you will enlighten them and help them be still more successful.

Most of us don't get a lot of opportunities to present to this elite group, so when we do, we want to make the most of them. We want to be 100% on our game.

**I always did something that I was a little not ready to do. I think that, that is how you grow. When there's a moment of 'Wow, I'm not so sure that I can do this,' and you push through those moments, it's then that you have a breakthrough. Sometimes that's a sign that something really great is about to happen. You're about to grow and learn a lot more about yourself."**

– Marissa Mayer, former CEO, Yahoo
and senior executive, Google

## GOT GAME?

"You got game" – generally meaning a combination of remarkable skill, talent, good looks and je ne sais quoi – has become a popular catchphrase in recent years. We think it's a great way to think about the concept of "executive presence."

In the C-suite, we want to present our best professional self – someone who is confident, poised, gracious, interesting, humble, trustworthy, tenacious, knowledgeable, wise, approachable and engaging.

Perhaps also witty, refreshing and curious. Or introspective, reliable and unflappable.

To a good degree, you get to decide what your personal brand of executive presence looks like. But be sure it's genuine and consistent. Be aware of the "presence" you're projecting, and don't try to fake it. It takes conscientious work precisely because we're not talking about role-playing here. We're talking about making positive, lasting change.

Amy Cuddy says powerful presence "stems from believing in and trusting yourself – your real, honest feelings, values, and abilities."[1] That's important, especially in the C-suite, because if you don't trust yourself, how likely is it that your boss's boss will trust you? "We all face daunting moments that must be met with poise if we want to feel good about ourselves and make progress in our lives," Cuddy says. "When you are not present, people can tell. When you are, people respond."[2]

## LESS IS MORE

Writer Tom Wolfe calls the desire some people have to share everything they know with people who don't know "information compulsion."[23] We all can be guilty of this. We're proud of what we learn. We're passionate about our work.

But in the C-suite, less truly is more. The higher up we go in an organization, the busier we'll find people. Still, it's always tempting to share more than what's needed. You prepare exceptionally well. You have mounds of data you gathered – painstakingly – over a period of weeks or months. You want to be comprehensive. You want to demonstrate your knowledge, your preparedness ...

## Stop right there![4]

When we have an opportunity to communicate with this exalted group of Cs, what we ultimately present will most likely be a tiny fraction of what we know. What we say must be factual, relevant, clear, succinct and unwavering. We must add value. We must be aware of our audience's pain points. We can't raise questions and problems without viable solutions. We have to anticipate every possible question and objection.

No ifs, ands or buts. (Or ums, so's or uhs.)

Know your message. Deliver the message. This is not the time for suspense and surprise. Don't bury the lead. Say what's important. And say it upfront.

## REFLECTION:

Consider writing down some key takeaways.
How will your next presentation change?

## ADOPT A C-SUITE STRATEGY

Think executive summary. Your presentation to the C-suite generally should not take more than four to five minutes. Take the time to prepare a one- or two-page top-line report of findings and recommendations.

Sure, you may have a 300-page document and 100 slides to support your conclusions. But those don't come out of your briefcase unless or until a question is raised that demands you provide precise details.

When preparing your executive summary, answer the following questions on each issue or concern:

**Know your information inside and out. But let your listeners decide if they need to know more. If they do, they will ask for it.**

"They'll want you to get to the bottom line right away – and they often won't let you finish your shtick without interrupting," says Nancy Duarte in the *HBR Guide to Persuasive Presentations.* "Set expectations … Most executives will be patient for five minutes and let you present your main points well if they know they'll be able to ask questions fairly soon."[5]

Finally, as with any presentation, rehearse.

Executive presence and clarity of message will win the day.

Tim Reynolds (currently executive director of the Robert D. Walter Center for Strategic Leadership at Ohio University) is a long-time client and friend who spent a lot of years at Whirlpool as vice president of talent and organization development. Tim told us he noticed a distinct gap between early career, mid-career and senior professional that got in the way of some top talents' ability to present to the next-level audience, whether standing or sitting. When there is a lack of this ability, it can impact not only the execution of results but become career limiting to the individual.

Once when Tim was working on succession planning with the top levels of the organization, he encountered a situation where a mid-level individual wasn't going to be promoted. The woman was extremely competent and experienced but was unable to effectively deliver a message to the C-suite. Her superiors just didn't believe the woman was confident or credible enough for a more senior role. They did not see and appreciate her day-to-day work, which was understood and trusted by her colleagues.

Instead of going to someone else, the executive talent team – because Whirlpool is so keenly focused on talent development – decided to invest in this individual.

In fact, Tim asked Vautier Communications to work with this mid-level executive, which we did, from early morning to late evening on a Sunday.

She was coached on eye contact, balance, posture, message organization – the whole package. When she presented to a group of C-suite and board members the next week, Tim shared that everyone was blown away. They said they practically didn't recognize the woman. And she was given the promotion.

"Executive presence is a key competency for leaders," Tim says. "To be impactful and influential, your functional/technical skills and executive presence skills have to be in alignment."

More advice from Tim:

"When you're presenting to the C-suite, you don't have a whole lot of time.
More than likely, they know what you're going to say; they've received and
read your material in advance. They will direct your presentation.
Anticipate their questions and the points they will want to discuss.
When responding, cover the pertinent points effectively and fast.
This is not the time for drawn-out conversations.
Get very specific. Deliver to one set of eyes.
Use your hands above the table. (More often
than not, presentations are made from a sitting
position.) Focus on good posture.
Watch non-words and industry-speak."

The main thing, according to Tim – and we agree
 – is practice.

Tim likes to tell another story about an executive
coming into Whirlpool at a high level. In his first talk
to employees, the executive read from his notes.
The problem was he replaced a well-respected, charismatic leader who loved
to tell stories. "When this guy came up to the podium and looked down and
read his notes, he disappointed and quickly lost his audience," Tim says.
Understanding the culture of the crowd is something too many speakers
neglect to do.

"How you enter has a lot to do with how you're received," Tim adds. "In that
environment, being a dynamic presenter and storyteller had a lot to do with a
leader's success." The new executive was receptive to some coaching and took
the time to practice. Not surprisingly, things quickly turned around for him.

The moral of that story: Even high level executives have to work at it.

> **Just because you are CEO, don't think you have landed.
> You must continually increase your learning, the way
> you think, and the way you approach the organization.
> I've never forgotten that."**
> – Indra Nooyi, PepsiCO.

## 05

# GET ORGANIZED!

**J**

"For every minute
spent organizing,
an hour is earned.

- BENJAMIN FRANKLIN

**Want to hear a really long, rambling story
with no clear beginning, middle or end?**

**Right, neither do we.**

There's a reason we've all heard countless arguments for planning and
organizing. "By failing to prepare, you are preparing to fail" (Benjamin Franklin).
"It takes as much energy to wish as it does to plan" (Eleanor Roosevelt).
"If you don't know where you are going, you'll end up someplace else"
(Yogi Berra). "Good order is the foundation of all things" (Edmund Burke).

Planning is simply essential if you want to accomplish something efficiently.

## START AT THE END

When planning and organizing formal remarks, our best advice is to employ a back to front technique. That may seem counterintuitive to some. But when you know where you want to finish, it's much easier to plot how you will get there.

Ask yourself: What do I need to convey to this audience? What do I want my net takeaway to be? What do I want them to do or know when I am finished? Write down the last sentence or two of your presentation before you do anything else. In writing that "finish," you've put yourself in a good position to write your opening.

## CRAFT AN IRRESISTIBLE BEGINNING

Many people struggle with that opening line. Understandably so; it's important. You want to capture the audience's attention quickly so they put away their phones, put aside lingering thoughts from their previous meeting and temporarily forget their next looming deadline. You want to earn their immediate respect and trust. Maybe even dazzle them.

**Never say anything, however, that isn't authentically you.**

You might consider starting with a stunning fact or juicy piece of data. You might use a thought-provoking quote or question. You could share a true and relevant story, share a surprising anecdote, or – if you have the skill – tell a joke. In that first 30 seconds, you want your audience to tune in, not out.

Stuck? We always recommend going to the source for more insight into your audience. Ask the person who extended the speaking invitation what the audience expects and wants to hear. You might be surprised by what you learn, and how this will enable you to customize your presentation – particularly your opening.

Still stuck? Just start writing. It will come. And you can fix it later during the editing process – which, by the way, should be given appropriate time in your schedule. This is when the really good writing and ideas come. It's not at all uncommon to throw away the first several paragraphs, bullets or slides, several times.

# MAKE THE MIDDLE SIZZLE, SING AND **SPEAK**

Once the closing and opening pieces are drafted, fill in the middle with clear, compelling arguments that build your case. Three is often considered the magic number in speech delivery, but you can incorporate two or four or five ideas. Together, the points you make should take your listeners with you, logically, so they arrive with you at the end. Everything you say should support your end goal or thesis.

We often refer to the content of a speech or presentation as "Forms of Influence" or "SPEAK." SPEAK is an acronym we use to represent six major content elements:

**S**tatistics and facts

**P**ersonal experience

**E**xamples

**A**nalogies

**K**iller quotes (or the quotable sound bite)

Employing these techniques will add interest, credibility and energy to your remarks.

One of the most popular TED Talks of 2017 was given by Shawn Achor, CEO of GoodThink Inc. The talk was called "The Happy Secret to Better Work." A Harvard graduate, Shawn researches and teaches positive psychology for a living, so he had plenty of scientific data to make his case. But he spent the first three minutes of his 12-minute talk sharing a personal story, a hilarious personal story. And that made his talk special and memorable. Shawn went on to incorporate all the other elements of SPEAK into his aspirational presentation, as do most of the top-ranking TED speakers. He asks compelling questions, shares fascinating insights and data, puts forth his unexpected hypothesis with supportive examples, shares his vision, challenges us with practical to-do's to advance that vision ... all while endearing himself to us and making us laugh out loud.

We encourage you to watch. Shawn's "happiness advantage" is something you'll enjoy thinking about and sharing with friends, family and colleagues. (Spoiler alert: 90% of long-term happiness is predicted not by the external world but by the way your brain processes the world; 75% of job success is predicted not by IQ, but by optimism, social support and the ability to see stress as a challenge instead of a threat. If that doesn't make a case for "don't worry; be happy!" then I don't know what does!)

If you're not a regular TED Talk viewer, you might think about subscribing. At least take a look at some of the most popular talks – any that catch your interest. You can learn a lot about how to organize, as well as deliver, a presentation by watching these standout examples.

 **Out of clutter find simplicity."**

– Albert Einstein

## WHAT TED SAYS ABOUT ORGANIZATION

"To provide an effective talk, you must slash back the range of topics you will cover to a single, connected thread – a throughline that can be properly developed," says TED head Chris Anderson. "Author Richard Bach said, 'Great writing is all about the power of the deleted word.' It's true of speaking too. The secret of successful talks often lies in what is left out. Less can be more."[1]

Anderson warns there's a right way and a wrong way to shorten your remarks:

There's a drastic consequence when you rush through multiple topics in summary form. They don't land with any force. You know the context ... But for the audience, which is coming to your work fresh, the talk will probably come across as conceptual, dry or superficial. It's a simple equation. Overstuffed equals underexplained. To say something interesting you have to take the time to do at least two things:

- **Show why it matters ... What's the question you're trying to answer, the problem you're trying to solve, the experience you're trying to share?**

- **Flesh out each point you make with real examples, stories and facts.[2]**

## ORGANIZE FOR IMPACT

Most presentations given to professional audiences fall into one of two categories:

**1** You want your audience to **DO** something, so you need to recommend, propose, persuade or influence.

**2** You want your audience to **KNOW** something, so you need to inform, update or educate.

If you want the audience to **DO** something, consider formatting your presentation as follows:

---

### Executive Summary (preferred format for the C-suite)

**Recommendation**
Here's what I'm recommending we do about the problem/opportunity.

**Options Considered**
Here are the other options I considered.

**Why (Implications)**
Here's why I went with the recommendation I did.

**Decision Points**
These are the decision points I need from you to move ahead.

**Next Steps**
These will be the next steps in the process once I get the OK.

---

Consider using our "Do This" tool to help you organize your presentation. Keep in mind, each box can include a bucket of slides or information.

## "Build" Format

### Situation

State the opportunity or problem.

### Recommendation

Offer your recommendation/solution to the problem or opportunity.

### Benefits

How does this benefit the audience? If there isn't a benefit to them, do they really want to change?

### Evidence/Support (SPEAK)

Use SPEAK to support your recommendation/solution.

### Summary

If you've gone a little long, you can choose to summarize prior to giving the ask.

### Action

Include calendar action step or the ask: Who, Does What, By When?

---

$\bigvee$ V A U T I E R
COMMUNICATIONS

**Do This**: Recommend, Propose, Persuade, Influence

**Audience** : _____

When done presenting, I want the Audience to **Do**:

| (Optional) Executive Summary | Situation Opportunity or Problem | Do This: Recommend or Propose | Benefits |
|---|---|---|---|
| **Executive Summary** ☐ Recommendation ☐ Options Considered ☐ Why ☐ Decision Points ☐ Next Steps | ☐ ☐ ☐ | ☐ ☐ ☐ | ☐ ☐ ☐ |

| Evidence: Support Do This | Evidence: Support Do This | Summary | Action |
|---|---|---|---|
| ☐ ☐ ☐ | ☐ ☐ ☐ | Situation ☐ Do This ☐ Benefits ☐ | Who ☐ Does What ☐ By When ☐ |

| Evidence S-P-E-A-K | Statistics & Facts | Personal Experience Demonstration | Example | Analogy | Killer Quote |
|---|---|---|---|---|---|

John

45

If you want the audience to **KNOW** something, you might consider the following organization:

**BAR (Storytelling)**

**Background**

Set up the story. Who's who, what do they want, what's getting in their way?

**Action**

AKA "the climax." What happens to the main character/characters?

**Result**

How does the story end? What was the lesson learned? Why are you telling this story? Be sure you have a clear connection between the story and the point of your presentation. Otherwise, it's a good story told in an inappropriate place.

**Build Format**

**Tell them what you're going to tell them.**

Think of this as an agenda and why it's important for the audience to hear.

**Tell them.**

Give them the details around the agenda pieces and add any SPEAK you may have.

**Tell them what you told them.**

Summarize what you've told them, why it's important and next steps.

Consider using our "Know This" format for organizing
the KNOW content/message.

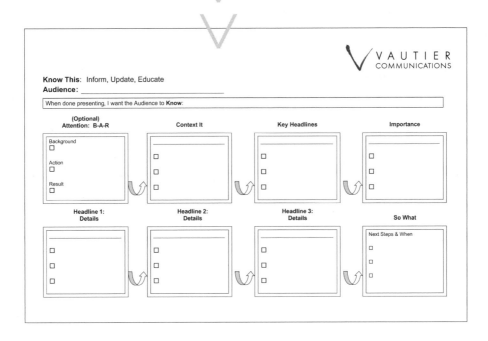

What's most important is to organize your presentation for clarity, conciseness
and relevance. Put yourself in your audience's shoes. Answer the questions they
care about: What, so what, how and how much?

# EXERCISE: ORGANIZE!

Organize your next presentation using one of the organizational outlines
provided here. If you don't have a meeting scheduled, invent a scenario or use
content from an old speech to see how the outlines might work for you.
Adjust as necessary. And if these formats don't work well for you, find another
one that does. You have to be comfortable.

# 06

UNDERSTAND WHAT THEY
SEE AND THINK;

## SKILLS

**J**

MANAGE WHAT THEY
HEAR AND BELIEVE

We're double teaming you on this chapter.

We call it our skills chapter.

Jenn will cover the first "What They See" portion of the discussion, and John will follow with "What They Hear."

Both are important and covered in some depth.

WHAT THEY SEE

**Research shows that when your verbal and nonverbal signals are out of alignment, people are forced to choose between what they hear and what they see."**

– Carol Kinsey Goman

We videotape everyone we coach because it is the easiest, quickest and most effective way for people to improve their presentation skills.

A speaker needs to see what her audience sees. (She also needs to hear what the audience hears, but we'll cover that a little later.)

Our best tip: Always incorporate video into your practice. It's so easy with our mobile devices. Ideally, ask someone else to videotape you, but if that's not possible, do it yourself. Very quickly, you'll see what your eyes, feet, hands – your entire body – are doing. Minor adjustments can have a huge impact on how you're perceived.

We share best practices and our own experiences and observations here, but readers should recognize there are exceptions to every rule. Ultimately, you get to decide what your audience will see and hear when you present.

And remember, what the audience doesn't see doesn't count. "Freshman" speakers are often surprised to learn that the extreme nervousness they feel on the inside often doesn't show up on the outside. If you avoid the telltale signs – tapping feet, eyes glued to floor, clenched fists, non-words – your audience will never guess you are anything but confident.

What you wear and your general grooming come into play, too, of course. But we covered that in Chapter Two.

## THE EYES HAVE IT

Establishing eye contact is the single most important thing you can do to establish trust. If you are looking down at the podium or up at the ceiling or at multiple people all over the room, you may will appear nervous, uncertain or untrustworthy. If you systematically look at one person, then another, and then another in a linear fashion, you may appear mechanical; your audience might view you as disingenuous.

We recommend making eye contact with one person as you begin and end one complete sentence or idea. Then, as necessary, pause briefly to gather your thoughts. When you need to, glance silently at your notes, laptop screen or projected slides to remind yourself of the next point you want to make. Then look up at a fresh set of eyes. Focus on that individual until you've completed your thought. Then go to the next person and your next thought. Try to connect with a set of eyes on the right side of the room, center and left, front and back, in random order. This may feel awkward at first but it becomes easy with practice.

Most importantly, you will look natural, confident and accessible to your audience. Try the focus exercise below and see how you do.

 **Stand up straight and realize who you are, that you tower over your circumstances."**

– Maya Angelou

## EXERCISE: TALK TO THE ANIMALS

Practice this technique for 15-30 minutes in an empty conference room, classroom or dining room. Line up at least eight empty chairs – or better yet, find staff or family members to sit in them. Then deliver lines from your favorite song, poem or speech – one line at a time, focusing on a different chair with each delivered line. You can imagine this in your head all day long but you won't fully appreciate it until you do it, videotape it, watch it, critique it and do it again and again.

We've heard many people practice on their pets. Or use stuffed animals. That's good by us, too. The goal is to get comfortable transitioning from one set of eyes to another, without losing your train of thought and without using non-words. Get comfortable with the silent pause, and watch your credibility soar.

Being able to look decision makers in the eye is career-changing, according to Tim Reynolds. You'll remember Tim from Chapter Four. He left Whirlpool several years ago to serve as executive director of the Robert D. Walter Center for Strategic Leadership in the College of Business at Ohio University. Tim and his wife, Tammy, are, in fact, certified to teach the Vautier Communications Executive Presence course.

Students in Tim's course visit and secure internships and jobs at companies like Google, Boeing, Nike and Dell. He says employers regularly comment the students have a "different level of maturity." Tim attributes this to their ability to make eye contact and to stand up (or sit up straight) and deliver confidently. They practice the skills.

"We get them in front of a lot of company teams so it's not their first rodeo when they have to deliver a message that counts," Tim admits. Many of his students, he says, have absolutely transformed their style of speech and executive presence inside a year. A junior in OU's leadership program, for example, was determined to compete for a position at Whirlpool that always had been reserved for graduate-level students. She was required to give a 20-minute presentation of her summer project and handle a tough Q&A. She put in the time and "she just crushed it," Tim says. "The point is, all of us can get better by simply cleaning up little things. You have to think of it as polishing a diamond."

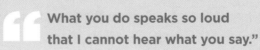

**What you do speaks so loud that I cannot hear what you say."**

– Ralph Waldo Emerson

## SET YOUR SIGHTS ON AMAZING GRACE

Your posture is also very important to how you're perceived. You want to appear poised and confident.

But "people make the mistake of over-weighting the importance of expressing strength, at the expense of warmth and trustworthiness," cautions Amy Cuddy.[1]

Aspire to be graceful, instead. Grace is simple elegance, refinement of movement, poise, finesse, courteous goodwill, decorum, respect, tact. **Be graceful and you'll amaze.**

In your neutral, "go-to" position, you want to stand or sit with your back and neck in a straight line, your chest out, your abdomen in, and your arms at your side (when standing) or on the table, palms down (when sitting). Your feet should be flat on the floor.

New Zealand physiotherapist Steve August, who has been studying what he refers to as the iHunch, says perfect posture is when the earlobe sits vertically above the point of the shoulder.[2] That's a great way to think about your posture.

Then, as you speak, you will naturally (or with practice) walk and gesture to illustrate or emphasize points you're making.

You don't want to be constantly moving, but you also don't want to stand motionless in one spot during your entire speech or presentation. Step forward or to the side, but when you do, be sure to finish the step. Don't rest in a half-step stance. And walk in the direction you're looking.

"Expansive body language increases our feelings of physical strength and skill," concludes Amy Cuddy in her research. "Contractive body language decreases them." She says: "Expanding your body physiologically prepares you to be present; it overrides your instinct to fight or flee, allowing you to be grounded, open, and engaged."[3]

**A strong stance with deliberate movement gives you and your audience a sense of calm, confidence and optimism.** Cuddy calls it "power posing."[4]

What you don't want to do? Sway, rock, lean, slouch, tap, shake, stretch, cower or otherwise appear unbalanced – unless it's part of your story. Unconscious movement detracts from your message.

Once again, this takes practice. It's not easy for most of us to control our nervous habits.

Here's a very easy and effective technique to employ at the start of your presentation or when you feel like you're losing your poise: Pause, take a breath, adjust your body so you're standing or sitting up straight and taking up some big space. Your audience won't notice, but in a few short seconds you will feel in control.


## HANDS WHERE I CAN SEE THEM

Incorporating gestures into formal or informal speaking is a great way to get and keep the audience's attention and to signal when you're going to tell them something especially important. You want to think about keeping your movement above your waist because your audience's eyes will go where they see movement.

As you move your arms or hands from a neutral position, you want to be sure to let them move freely and naturally. Don't lock your elbows to your waist (what we call the Velcro effect). There should be air between your arms and your torso. Think about making larger gestures (especially in a large room) so your audience can see them. Your arms should move outside of your shoulders and above your waist. When your arms are up and away from your body, you appear more expressive and engaging.

Avoid curling your hands or forming fists with them. The audience is likely to interpret this as anxiety, anger or closed-mindedness. They may even feel you aren't being truthful. You want people to see you as transparent, approachable and relaxed. By opening your hands, you open the door for people to hear you and trust what you're telling them.

Naturally, you don't want to overdo your body language. You don't want to appear as if you're going to fly away from all the arm flapping. Gesturing can be effective, but if you're out of breath and dripping sweat, you may be overdoing it. Too much of anything can be distracting. In point of fact, overdoing is extremely rare. Most people err on the side of not doing enough, or not doing anything at all. It takes practice to get it just right.

## WHEN ALL ELSE FAILS –
## AND EVEN WHEN IT DOESN'T – SMILE!

A smile may not always be appropriate but when it is, use it. Plenty of research studies prove the impact of a smile, and even attempt to put a dollar value to it – 16,000 pounds sterling cash, to be precise.[5] But our own personal experience tells us much more. A smile unarms. It relaxes. It forgives. It relates. It invites. It commiserates. It trusts. It connects.

All facial expressions are powerful. Use them freely, as long as they're genuine.

Need practice? Say cheeeeese!

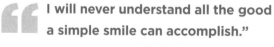 **I will never understand all the good a simple smile can accomplish."**
– Mother Teresa

WHAT THEY HEAR

**We often refuse to accept an idea
merely because the tone of voice in which it has
been expressed is unsympathetic to us."**

– Friedrich Nietzsche

The audio portion of your videotaped rehearsal is every bit as important as the visual. If your audience doesn't hear and understand your message, your magnificent posture and sublime eye contact won't mean a whole lot.

## VOLUME UP

One of the common problems we see when people present their ideas is volume. Most people speak far too softly. On rare occasions, we experience people speaking too loudly. So what is the best volume? Obviously, it does depend on the size of the audience and its distance from you. But generally, we say, on a scale of 1-10, with one being a whisper and 10 being a shout, you want to be at a seven or eight. It should feel a bit uncomfortable. When you are using a microphone, you'll still want to achieve that volume level, but will do so with a combination of your own vocal chords and the sound system in the room. That requires a rehearsal or two, ideally in the precise location where you'll be presenting.

**Bonus: When you turn your speaking voice up, you'll also turn up your confidence.**

## EXPRESS YOURSELF

Inflection also is important. **Listen** to me! See what I mean? When "listen" is emphasized, you really take note. It's important not to sound monotone or talk in a singsong fashion. Your audience will miss your key points, not remember what you said, or potentially fall asleep – if they opt to stick around at all. When you deliver remarks, think about changing the tone of your voice ... raising your voice to indicate a question, lowering it at the end of a sentence, speaking louder to express importance, excitement and certainty, and talking softer to express sadness, concern, acceptance or regret. Varying your pitch will help your audience stay focused on your message and increase their understanding.

Inflection is particularly effective if you're speaking with excitement and passion, and suddenly pause to lower your voice. When we speak softer, the recipient *must* listen more intently. This technique should be done sparingly and only when it makes sense or you'll lose the effect.

Need we say it? Do **not** speak with an upward inflection at the end of your sentences. It conveys uncertainty, not to mention it gets annoying pretty quickly. (For a bit of fun and to see what we mean, check out: https://www.youtube.com/watch?v=tqNhEzrWQpY.)

## EXERCISE: SAY IT HOW YOU MEAN IT

Read the following sentences aloud, putting the inflection on the bold word. Observe how the meaning of the sentence changes.

**He** thought the end of the speech was particularly strong for a first-time TED presenter.

He **thought** the end of the speech was particularly strong for a first-time TED presenter.

He thought the **end** of the speech was particularly strong for a first-time TED presenter.

He thought the end of the speech was particularly strong for a **first-time** TED presenter.

He thought the end of the speech was particularly strong for a first-time **TED** presenter.

**Given the choice between trivial material brilliantly told versus profound material badly told, an audience will always choose the trivial told brilliantly."**

– Robert McKee, *Story: Substance, Structure, Style, and the Principles of Screenwriting*

## DON'T UNDERESTIMATE THE POWER OF THE PAUSE

Your audience needs time to hear and process what you're saying.
Not to mention, the pregnant pause is powerful when interjected at the right time.
It says: "Pay attention to what I just said. Think about the impact. This matters to me; it should matter to you."

It also doesn't hurt to give yourself a second or two to catch your breath and collect your thoughts. The pause tells your audience you're confident and in control. Incorporate it into your presentations to your benefit.

## PACE TAKES PATIENCE

We all know people who talk way too fast or woefully slow. It's hard to stay with them and comprehend what they're saying. It's especially challenging during a formal speech or presentation.

While talking very slowly think (Mr. Rogers) or talking very quickly think (Shawn Achor in his TED Talk on *The Happy Secret to Better Work* mentioned earlier) can be effective, the vast majority of the time, you want to speak at a pace that's slightly slower than conversational. You especially want to slow it down when speaking to audiences that are older or for whom English is not a first language. In our diverse, global society, this is more often the case than not.

## NIX THE NON-WORDS, CLICHÉS AND JARGON

"Most students and even a lot of people at very high levels are guilty of using non-words," Tim Reynolds (our friend from Whirlpool and Ohio University) points out. "Getting rid of 'right,' 'you know,' 'as a matter of fact' language is big." It takes a lot of practice.

When you pause and find another set of eyes for your next message, you will find yourself injecting fewer ums, likes, uhs, reallys and so's. Those words – as well as clichés and industry-speak – water down the impact of your message. The surest way to avoid these speech-destroyers is to know your material well. Edit it to perfection. And then rehearse multiple times. I know we've said it before, but we can't emphasize enough the importance of practice. That's why we give it its own chapter.

**REFLECTION:**

What non-words, clichés and industry jargon will you commit to nixing?

One of our long-time clients, Mason, Ohio-based Cintas Corporation, provides a wide range of products and services to more than a million businesses to keep employees uniformed and the workplace safe and clean. Erin Miller, corporate director of human resources at Cintas, has put more than a thousand Cintas partners (employees) through our two-day program.

"To see someone who is timid and reserved and uncomfortable with public speaking literally transformed in such a short amount of time is incredible ... They learn it's OK to propel their voices, to use inflection ... but they also realize they can only do this effectively if they know the content ...With respect to pace, I don't like too slow or too quick. If you speak too slowly, you'll lose the audience. They'll take out their phones; they'll disengage. If you speak too quickly, they won't even be sure what you said. You need to know your audience and maintain the right pace for them. The C-suite wants quicker; the line wants it a little slower. Sometimes, I ask my audience for permission to go through some slides more quickly, when I feel it's a review of material most have seen ...

There is a leader in our organization who struggled with saying "um" all the time. It was very distracting. Some coaching helped him realize his problem stemmed from not knowing the material well. When he gave himself enough time to get comfortable with what he was saying, he all but eliminated the non-words from his presentations. You have to put in the preparation time."

Erin's best advice:

"Remember to breathe. Sometimes, it's just a matter of exhaling and resetting. I tell our partners to remember, it's just a conversation. Yes, there may be 100 people in the audience, but it's still just a conversation, so take it as that. You may stumble, but it's OK. Pause, reset and go forward."

## STORYTELLING IS (STILL) MAGIC

07

"There's always
room for a story that
can transport people
to another place."

– J.K. ROWLING

Storytelling became the new black in corporate communications sometime in the late 1980s or early 1990s. And it remains hugely popular – understandably and deservedly so. It's relatively easy (we've all been telling stories since we were small children) and extremely effective. Stories are relatable; they connect people through emotion, vulnerability and like-circumstances. They show how complex pieces fit together. They provide a visual and a vision. They entertain and inspire. They allow people to learn without feeling taught or manipulated. And they're sticky; people can remember them.

## BE A STUDENT OF STORY

Storytelling now can routinely be found in university catalogs and in business conference brochures. Books, articles and blog posts on the topic abound, and brands can't get their stories together and out fast enough. Since 1984, more than 100,000 students from around the globe have taken Robert McKee's famed seminars on storytelling, including Julia Roberts, David Bowie, Kirk Douglas, Jimmy Fallon and executives of Disney, Microsoft, Nike and Siemens.

Referred to by many of his students as "the Aristotle of our times," McKee will tell you: "Stories are how we remember; we tend to forget lists and bullet points. If a businessperson understands that his or her own mind naturally wants to frame experience in a story, the key to moving an audience is not to resist this impulse but to embrace it by telling a good story."[1]

McKee cautions, "You emphatically do not want to tell a beginning-to-end tale describing how results meet expectations. This is boring and banal. Instead, you want to display the struggle between expectation and reality in all its nastiness."[2]

Storytelling is arguably the most natural, time-tested and effective way to communicate, entertain, educate and persuade.

**The best speakers, president or Ph.D. chemist, lavishly illustrate their talks with short, striking vignettes. In fact, the most potent speeches are often little more than strings of such vignettes, loosely linked by an outline."**

– Tom Peters, author of *In Search of Excellence*

## AND WHAT MAKES A GOOD STORY?

The best stories are enthusiastically told. They engage, evolve, appeal to many, are without ego and without end. And, perhaps most importantly, they allow people, who may be skeptical of what you have to say, to do their own interpretations and draw their own conclusions.

Chris Anderson of TED says to do these four things when sharing a story:

**1** **Base it on a character your audience can empathize with.**

**2** **Build tension, whether through curiosity, social intrigue, or actual danger.**

**3** **Offer the right level of detail. Too littl e and the story is not vivid. Too much and it gets bogged down.**

**4** **End with a satisfying resolution, whether funny, moving, or revealing.**

He adds, "Of course, it's all in the execution."[3]

## One of My Favorite Stories

Nick is a friend and a wonderful coach at our CrossFit gym. He attended one of our presentation skills programs, as he's someone who loves to learn as much as he can in all different fields. He's what you think of when you hear the term "lifelong learner."

He's also a single dad to an 18-year-old son. A few years back, when his son was a preteen, he admitted their relationship became a bit strained. They just weren't connecting like they had previously.

Nick said he really wanted his son to come into the gym and get interested and excited about CrossFit. His son, on the other hand, was interested in video games and seemingly not much else. Nick forced his son to come to the gym one day and his son hated every second of it. He pulled back even more.

A few weeks go by and Nick wakes up one morning and tells himself that he has to try to find a way to connect with his son.

"He's an awesome kid and I want to get our relationship back," he told me. So he woke his son, sat him down in front of the TV and said, "All right, teach me how to play these video games." Nick invested hours learning the games and competing and laughing with his son.

A couple more weeks go by and his son ends up telling him he wants to start working out. Nick couldn't have been happier.

Years later, father and son are extremely close and they spend meaningful time doing all sorts of activities, including CrossFit classes and playing video games.

Finding common ground with your audience (and then meeting them halfway!) can be powerful.

## STORIES **JUST DO IT**

We've known since childhood that stories have a hero (the protagonist), a bad guy (the antagonist), struggles and setbacks (rising and falling action), and a conclusion (the denouement or payoff).

Many companies effectively use story in their branding to external audiences and now are also using it with great success inside their organizations.

"Our stories are not about extraordinary business plans or financial manipulations," explains Nelson Farris, Nike's director of corporate education and chief storyteller. "They're about people getting things done."[4]

Cofounders Phil Knight (runner) and Bill Bowerman (Knight's coach), along with Steve Prefontaine, the Olympic runner who was also coached by Bowerman, form Nike's heroic triad. Nike's antagonists are its competitors but also events like the 1975 car crash that ended Prefontaine's life.

"'Nike has made understanding its heritage an intrinsic part of its corporate culture," Farris explains. For example, there's the story of coach Bowerman creating Nike's famous waffle sole in his workshop with a waffle iron when he decided his team needed better shoes – a story that colorfully illustrates the company's history of innovation.[5]

Gatorade does a fabulous job telling stories of the everyday man/woman achieving in sports and fitness. Its Replay campaign told stories to support the message, "Once you're an athlete, you're always an athlete." Grab a tissue and watch: https://www.youtube.com/watch?v=fMl3ktiOnrY.

The Michigan Economic Development Corporation tells stories of Pure Michigan – family adventure in pristine nature. Farmers Insurance tells outlandish (but true) stories to illustrate they'll cover just about anything. Hallmark tells touching stories of friend and family reunions, achievements and weathering tough times. The examples are almost endless – because stories work. They tug at a person. They facilitate connections. They strengthen relationships. And they are memorable.

> **It is more fun to talk with someone who doesn't use long, difficult words but rather short, easy words like, 'what about lunch?'"**
>
> – A. A. Milne

## WHAT IF STORYTELLING ISN'T IN MY DNA?

We all have stories, although admittedly, storytelling comes more easily to some than others. Being curious helps. Reading helps. All your life experiences help.

There's a book we like to recommend by Daniel Coyle called *The Little Book of Talent*. Coyle's number one tip for developing any talent is to "stare at who you want to become." He doesn't mean passively watching. When he says staring, he means "the kind of raw, unblinking, intensely absorbed gazes you see in hungry cats or newborn babies."[6]

### GO STARE.

One way to get ideas for stories is to watch and/or listen to others tell them. The online TED library is a fabulous place to find stellar storytellers; there are seemingly endless examples there.

You'll notice that some stories are stretches, and may seem to have very little to do with the topic at first blush. But a creative storyteller will make the connection for his listeners.

Another way to find a story is brainstorming. Ask yourself a whole lot of story-creation questions. What does the protagonist of my story want, who or what is keeping this from happening, what action was or will be taken to conquer evil (or overcome obstacles)?

"'Desire is the blood of a story," says McKee. "Desire is not a shopping list but a core need that, if satisfied, would stop the story in its tracks.'"[7] Name your protagonist's (and antagonist's) desire.

## Other questions to consider:

Who is my audience?

What am I passionate about? (It's important to care deeply about what you're presenting.)

What does my audience expect? What do they really want from me? What is their likely mood and point of view on my topic?

Why should they care what I have to say? What emotion can I appeal to?

What do I want the audience to take away? What change must take place in their minds?

How will I build my case? Where will my audience be physically and emotionally, at the start of my presentation? How will I move them to where I need them to be?

How can I build suspense, excitement, interest?

What's at risk? What would happen if the audience didn't come along with me and believe, say or do what I want them to?

How can/will this conversation make the world better?

What are my biggest hurdles? How can I overcome objections?

What current or historic event is similar to what I want to speak about?

What part of my own personal story and set of experiences is most relevant here?

What's funny? Can/should I make light of the situation?

How much time do I have?

What accompanying visuals, audio or props would help tell the story?

Finally, once your story is drafted, you need to ask yourself if it is an honest telling. McKee advises storytellers to make certain there is "'neither an exaggeration nor a soft-soaping of the struggle.'"[8]

Here are some excellent Do's and Don'ts from storytelling scholar Annette Simmons:

> **Don't** act superior. Let your audience think for themselves.

> **Don't** bore your listeners. Get specific. Don't wander into hypotheticals. Don't ramble. No, really, stop talking!

> **Don't** scare people or make them feel guilty.

> **Do** connect at the level of humanity. Share a funny or vulnerable moment. What do you hate, love, admire, long for, fear and mourn that you know your audience will, too? "The best thing you have going for you as a storyteller is that you're a human being."

> **Do** leave them feeling hopeful "for a future that is reachable, worth their effort, or both."[9]

Charts and graphs have their place. But even the most analytical of audiences want stories. Learn to share stories and the world will open up to you.

# REFLECTION AND BRAINSTORMING:

## WHAT STORIES CAN YOU TELL?

**1.** Name up to three of your all-time favorite stories. They can be from novels or film, childhood tales, favorite family memories, comic strips, speeches you've heard ... Think about why they are at the top of your list. What elements of these stories can you employ in the telling of your own? Jot down ideas for your next presentation.

**2.** Thinking about a specific past or future presentation, answer some of the story-creation questions we proposed in this chapter. Then get your creative juices going – however you're accustomed to doing that. One way: Brainstorm as fast as you can; no second guessing or editing allowed until you have 50 thought-starters. Take your best 10 and develop them further.

## 08

## GOT DATA?
## MAKE IT SIZZLE AND POP!

"Almost every
PowerPoint presentation
sucks rotten eggs."

— SETH GODIN

There is no one best way to give a speech in a large auditorium. Nor is there one way to present material in a conference room. Many factors will determine your format:

- **Your objective (s)**

- **Your own personal style and comfort level as a presenter**

- **The size and makeup of the audience**

- **The complexity and weightiness of the material presented**

- **Time allotted and the size and shape of the room**

- **Availability of audiovisual equipment and content**

All of these considerations should be weighed before deciding the approach you will take.

In this chapter, we want to briefly discuss some format options and then focus on the formal presentation, which affords the opportunity to incorporate audio and visual effects, such as slides, video and props into your talk.

## CHOOSE ONE OF FOUR FORMAT TYPES

### Extemporaneous Remarks

While you can't prepare for these in the same way you can a planned talk, you can invest in building your executive presence, practicing your presentation skills and finessing your personal stories so when opportunities come along, you are comfortable delivering on message. As Mark Twain is purported to have said, "It usually takes me more than three weeks to prepare a good impromptu speech." Anticipate topics you will be asked about and consider outlining your key thoughts. Many companies prepare message platforms or "trees" for executives by topic area. Know your positions on important issues and be prepared with three points to back up each one of them.

### Informal Speech

We offer a tool called Speak from Notes™ to help presenters sequence their thoughts effectively. It's based on the presenting-from-index-card idea. This method keeps you organized in both the development and delivery of your content. We're happy to provide Speak from Notes complimentarily to program participants and readers of this book. Just ask us!

Another good option for informal speeches is a "follow-along" handout.

## Semiformal Discussion

Examples of semiformal events might be "softball" media interviews, one-on-one meetings, social media video spots, internal podcasts, team meetings or webinars. In these cases, you're often representing your company's point of view, not just your own. Most companies have policies in place for these types of opportunities. It is best to get advice and coaching from your internal communications pros. At minimum, know your audience, your objective, the key points you want to make and the potential objections to your point of view before you start talking.

## Formal Presentation

When you are standing up in front of a group – or sitting at a conference room table for an important presentation – executive presence is particularly important. You want to know your content well and present it flawlessly. But you also want to be perceived as confident, credible and capable. You want people to listen with respect and trust you. All the techniques we talked about in previous chapters will come into play here: good eye contact, posture, volume, inflection, movement and gestures, the idea of talking about something you care deeply about, storytelling, and practice, practice, practice.

Without question, the addition of slides or even video, audio effects and props can make your presentation much more interesting to your audience. When your presentation is complex, detailed or lengthy, slides can help you stay on track. They serve as visual reminders of what you want to say next. They also help your audience remain focused and engaged.

However (it's worth saying again), **DO NOT READ YOUR SLIDES.** It is an insult to your audience.

**The art of simplicity is a puzzle of complexity."**

– Douglas Horton

## TEN SURE WAYS TO NOT SUCK

We couldn't put Seth Godin's quote out there and leave you hanging. Regardless of the tools and technology you use – PowerPoint, Prezi, whiteboard, tablet, teleprompter, telepresence – follow these guidelines and we guarantee your presentation won't suck like rotten eggs:

**1** Keep it simple and clean. Utilize space to give your audience's eyes a rest and help them focus. Limit text and bullet points, and avoid distracting patterns, colors and animation. Less is definitely more.

**2** Demonstrate you know your audience. Make it relevant. Personalize if possible.

**3** Keep it real. Be authentic. Show concrete examples your audience can relate to.

**4** Find ways for the audience to interact. For instance, ask questions before revealing the data you collected. Mix it up – within reason. Change the pace. Incorporate video clips, audio clips and animation; use a whiteboard or posters; or bring out a prop to illustrate your points.

**5** Use high-quality graphics – pictures (each is worth a thousand words!), charts and graphs vs. blocks of text or numbers.

**6** Be original. Avoid the templated backgrounds, clipart and the cheesy sounds and images that come with presentation software. Consider props and audio – rarely used but so effective, particularly because they aren't expected.

**7** Make it readable. Consider the size of your audience and where your audience will be. Be sure there's good contrast so they can see without straining.

**8** Be consistent. Do not vary type fonts and backgrounds too much. We recommend one font for headers, one font for text and no more than three backgrounds.

**9** Make an extra copy of your final slide, absent any animation you may have incorporated. That way, if you accidentally click past the end of your presentation, your audience won't realize it. You want to end the way you want to end, versus going dark.

**10** Be prepared for anything. Remember, the more technology and other "extras" you incorporate, the more that could go wrong. Practice with and test all your equipment – ideally in the room you will be using. Bring an extra electronic copy and hard copy of your presentation. Consider extra batteries, power cords and extension cords. Be ready to present without your visuals if the dreaded unexpected occurs.

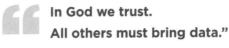

**In God we trust.
All others must bring data."**
– W. Edwards Deming

## THE FEELING BEHIND YOUR EYES

There are a number of fabulous books out there on presentation design. We provide the names of a few in our recommended reading section at the end of this book. We encourage you and/or your graphics, communications and administrative teams to spend some time with them.

In his gorgeous book, Good Charts, Scott Berinato (managing editor of *Harvard Business Review* and self-described DataViz geek) makes the point that we should trust "the feeling behind our eyes." The goal is not perfection, but rather balance. There isn't any particular magic about colors or size or numbers of tick marks. Just ask yourself, "Does it look neat and clean, or messy and muddled?" Berinato does acknowledge that consistent structure is important. Every chart, he says, should include a title, subtitle, visual field and source line.[1]

We can't resist sharing this brilliant technique from *Good Charts:* George Alvarez, a Harvard professor, was giving a lecture one day and noticed students were fixated on his charts – even when he moved on to another topic entirely. So he shut the screen off. "The effect was stunning. Eyes that had been fixed on the picture darted to him and locked in. With nothing else to look at, the students listened intently."[2]

Mix it up. Experiment. Keep pushing for the aha! There isn't one solution for every situation. Know your audience and pay close attention to that feeling behind your eyes.

# EXERCISE AND REFLECTION

Take out your next or last presentation deck. Is there an opportunity to survey or otherwise engage the audience? Challenge yourself to remove text from each slide. What else can you do to increase the white or negative space on each slide? Would pictures or graphs better convey some messages? What more can you do to make your presentation attractive to the eye? Consider consulting a designer or your marketing/creative department.

John

## CREATE AND COMMIT
## TO A PRACTICE STRATEGY

09

"It is a mistake to think that
the practice of my art has
become easy to me. I assure you,
dear friend, no one has given
so much care to the study of
composition as I. There is
scarcely a famous master in
music whose works I have not
frequently and diligently studied."

– WOLFGANG AMADEUS MOZART

The secret you've been waiting for ... Are you ready for it?

The way to get over any fear you may have of public speaking and delivering C-suite presentations is ... practice. That's it.

When you know your material well and you practice presenting it, you will be amazed at how easy it becomes and how effective you will be.

Don't expect speaking success to magically come your way as you advance in your career.

As much as we encourage speakers to appear natural, there is nothing natural about public speaking.

**No one is a natural presenter. Everyone has to work at it.**

Sure, some may have more interest and ability. They may have a more outgoing personality and sense of humor that propels them forward. But trust us: Anyone who is any good at speaking has put in the time.

Do yourself the favor of preparing your remarks well in advance of your meeting or event, when possible. We know everyone is short on time. Sometimes you won't have material until a day or two before you have to present it. But do everything in your power to give yourself the time to practice. It will make all the difference!

When you ask people who are in positions of evaluating speakers what the most important presentation skill or technique is, they will tell you, "It's knowing the content." Period. End of discussion. Only if you know your content can you begin to incorporate other best practices of public speaking. And, when you know your content well, you will automatically speak with much more confidence and enthusiasm.

## PRACTICE. PRACTICE. PRACTICE. REPEAT.

In their book, *Creative Confidence*, David Kelley (founder of IDEO, a global design and innovation company) and Tom Kelley (IDEO partner and author of *The Art of Innovation*) make the point that throughout our lives, we do all kinds of "scary" things that become not so scary as soon as we do them, like riding a bike, jumping off a diving board or trying strange new food. Yet, despite those successful experiences, we cling to our fears whenever we encounter unfamiliar territory. Almost anyone can apply a can-do mindset to the challenges before them, according to the Kelleys. What matters most, they say, is "your belief in your capacity to create positive change and the courage to take action."[1]

Unfortunately, public speaking is at the top of most people's list of scary things. And the longer people avoid it, the more the fear seems to grow. What we find helpful is to think of public speaking as simply having a conversation about something you know well and are passionate about – usually with people who very much want to hear your point of view. We love Hungarian novelist George Konrad's famous quote: "Courage is only the accumulation of small steps." We just need to begin to walk. And then continue down the path.

## DIFFERENT STROKES FOR DIFFERENT FOLKS

Just as people prefer one format over another, speakers tend to have different practice strategies. What's important is that you practice. And choose a structure that's right for you.

Marshall Goldsmith has observed that "imposing structure ... is how we seize control of our otherwise unruly environment ... Successful people know all this intuitively ... But for the simple task of interacting with other people, we prefer to wing it."[2] We don't want to admit we need the help. We reason that we've achieved success in our personal lives and careers; we shouldn't need help communicating. Yet, we most certainly do. All of us.

Develop the practice structure you like, but don't do yourself or your audience the disservice of "winging it." Following are some options to consider.

## DON'T OVER-COMPLICATE IT

If you organize your presentation logically and think of it in terms of key themes or points, you will have a much easier time remembering what you want to say. While most presenters don't memorize their entire speech, most competent speakers get very familiar with the opening and closing points. Your slides or notes can serve as prompts for the content in between.

## CHUNK IT OUT

One method of practice we like to recommend involves piecing out your talk. Develop your remarks a couple of weeks prior to the event, if possible. Then, each day leading up to your presentation, read and commit to memory one "chunk" of your presentation. You can invest as little as 10 minutes per day. We've seen this system work very effectively for most of the people we coach.

## EMBRACE REPETITION

This is Tip #43 from Daniel Coyle's *Little Book of Talent*: Coyle gives the example of the accuracy achieved by pro golfers who practice the same swing over and over again. That's the only way to achieve the consistency and confidence they have to have. Instead of viewing repetition as a chore, Coyle says, we should view it as a powerful tool. He quotes martial artist and actor Bruce Lee: "I fear not the man who has practiced ten thousand kicks once, but I fear the man who has practiced one kick a thousand times."[3]

Coyle's Tip #44 is to have a blue-collar mindset. That is, get up and go to work at it, whether you feel like it or not. And Coyle's Tip #45 is to spend at least five hours of practice for every one hour of performance. "A five-to-one ratio of practice time to performance time is a good starting point; ten to one is even better," he says.[4]

## SAY IT OUT LOUD

We strongly urge you to go through your speech or presentation in its entirety at least three times before you deliver it to your intended audience. Ideally, one of those practice sessions will be a dress rehearsal in the venue where you will present – or as close to that scenario as you can manage. We recognize this isn't always practical, but do make a point of delivering your talk out loud in at least one of your practice sessions. Reading your presentation silently does not have the same benefit.

For at least one of your rehearsals, try to arrange for someone to listen to your talk and provide feedback. And, as mentioned earlier, consider videotaping yourself.

**Champions keep playing until they get it right."**

– Billie Jean King

# EXERCISE AND REFLECTION

What strategies have worked for you – or not worked for you – in the past? Consider asking people whose presentations you admire how they prepare. Create (or refine) your own personal practice strategy. Commit to using it consistently, understanding that you can tweak it as you go.

## MADE IT TO THE C-SUITE? YOU STILL NEED TO PRACTICE.

We talked to our client Chuck Bogosta, who, as you may remember from Chapter 3, is president of both UPMC International and UPMC Hillman Cancer Center. In his roles, he routinely presents in front of large, international audiences. Even though he is an experienced leader and accomplished presenter, he rehearses his remarks each and every time.

"What works for me is writing out what I want to say. Typically, I'll ask my team to draft something but I actively edit and take notes. I think through every possible question I may be asked and either address it in the presentation (that's preferable and most often the case) or, if I'm hoping I don't get asked the question, I'll prepare separately and thoroughly so I'm in the best possible position to respond if the issue does come up ...

I attempt to encapsulate what I'm going to cover with each slide. That process helps me commit what I'm going to say to memory. I go through the deck the night before a presentation (generally talking out loud) and again the day of the presentation. So by the time I get in front of my audience, I'm very familiar with the content and know precisely how I want to deliver it. I also make sure I'm completely familiar with the AV, where I'll be standing, and where the audience is. And then I just try to be myself. I try to be as relaxed and genuine as I can be."

Chuck was gracious to also share an example of a presentation gone awry. He had invited a department leader to present to a group that included the organization's chairman. The presenter had about 20 slides and read each one of them, verbatim, very mechanically, and in an awkward, nervous tone, with long pregnant pauses. It made everyone in the room uncomfortable. The chairman politely excused himself as soon as the presentation was over. It was clear to everyone that the department head wasn't comfortable with the content or with presenting. It was a huge missed opportunity for her.

"I don't know anyone who wants to get in a room and listen to someone who could have benefited from intense training," Chuck says. "We try to make sure our people can carry the room," he says. "It involves asking questions, being able to lighten the mood and getting people to like you."

**A lot of people want to find a shortcut.
I find the best shortcut is the long way, which is basically
two words: hard work."**  – Randy Pausch
*The Last Lecture*

Note: Randy Pausch, diagnosed with terminal cancer, gave his last lecture to students at Carnegie Mellon in 2007. When asked his secret to getting early tenure, he said, "It's pretty simple. Call me any Friday night in my office at ten o'clock and I'll tell you."

## DO THE **REPS**

We want to return to Daniel Coyle's *Little Book of Talent* a final time.
In choosing your practice strategy, he suggests applying a REPS gauge.

Does your method meet these criteria?

**Reaching and repeating –** Does the practice have you operating on the edge of your ability, reaching and repeating?

**Engagement –** Is the practice immersive? Does it command your attention? Does it use emotion to propel you toward a goal?

**Purposefulness –** Does the task directly connect to the skill you want to build?

**Strong, speedy feedback –** Does the learner receive a stream of accurate information about his performance, where he succeeded and where he made mistakes?[5]

Practice doesn't necessarily make perfect, but it will dramatically improve your game. Don't view it as an option or a luxury. It's a must-do.

# 10

## WRITING TO INFORM, PERSUADE AND INSPIRE

"Je ne vois qu'une règle:
être clair. Si je ne suis
pas clair, tout mon monde
est anéanti."

Translation: "I see but one rule: to be clear.
If I am not clear, all my world crumbles to nothing.

—MARIE-HENRI BEYLE DIT STENDHAL,
WRITING TO BALZAC

Executive presence is more than how you enter a room and present yourself visually and verbally. You also must appear confident, poised, smart and trustworthy – on the page.

Our advice: Write simply and succinctly.

It's tempting to end this chapter right there.

**But we know writing simply is not as simple as it sounds.**

## THE WHY OF WRITING WELL

Before we dig into the "how" of writing well, let's spend a minute on the "why."

Clear, concise writing results in more accurate communication, which generally means fewer questions, less follow-up, faster responses and more decisions being made in our favor.

The most common mistakes we see in professional writing stem from unnecessary complexity, archaic formality, verbosity, and over-use of hyperbole, clichés and jargon. Big words and long sentences will not impress someone with limited time and a lot of responsibilities and distractions.

Before you begin writing, ask yourself, "What do I want my audience to know, think or do as a result of this communication?" Then help them get there with as few words as possible.

Be transparent. Eliminate the unnecessary.

As Joseph Williams and Gregory Colomb say in their standout book, *Style:* "Of the many graces of style, the compression of a snail is still ... the first."[1]

 **The very word is like a bell."**
– John Keats

## ARE YOU FEELIN' THE DRAFT?

Even the best writers – check that, *especially* the best writers – know the writing process requires several drafts. If writing presents a challenge for you, write the way you talk. Just get something down on the page. Then, allow time for massaging – that is, reworking and proofing. Examine every sentence and every word. Is this *precisely* what you mean to say?

Once your first draft is written, check for tone. Is there room for misinterpretation? Could your words offend? Tone is critically important in business writing. The simpler your writing, the less chance your tone will be misunderstood. It's usually best, especially when you don't know your audience well, to avoid attempts at humor or sarcasm. Be short, but not curt.

The goal should be to "craft prose so quick, silken, and natural that the reader understands it immediately and with a single reading," says Paula LaRocque, one of our favorite writers on writing and a former managing editor of the *Dallas Morning News.* There should be "no need to go back and re-read," LaRocque says. "No need (for the reader) to do the writer's work."[2]

Ideally, let important reports, speeches, blog posts and even emails sit for a period of time. You'll be amazed at how different your writing will read when you come back to it later. We can almost guarantee you, you'll want to change something, and that "something" will make the writing more effective. This is especially the case when you are emotional (angry, disappointed, sad, surprised, tired, thrilled) or the topic is sensitive or complex.

"If we are socially responsible writers, we should make our ideas no simpler than they deserve, but no more difficult than they have to be," say Williams and Colomb, in writing about the ethics of writing style.[3] They aptly suggest, "Write to others as you would have others write to you."[4] If the receiver of our message concludes we're careless, lazy or self-indulgent, it's unlikely they'll want to have anything to do with us.

Take the time to get it right and, we promise you, you will be rewarded.

## USE THE TOOLS AVAILABLE TO YOU

Good writing gives power and relevance to ideas. Too often, we fail to recognize its importance and give it the time and attention it deserves.

Using the precise word, versus the first word that comes to mind, can change outcomes. Think of it this way: You're investing the time to write something; why not spend a few more minutes to craft it in a way that is much more likely to accomplish your objective?

Contrary to what some people may think, dictionaries and thesauruses are not for wimps, nor are they only for professional writers. They are truly valuable tools for every business communicator.

If you have any doubt about the mechanics of your writing, refer to a style manual – another still-fashionable tool. The most common and well-respected style guides are Associated Press (AP), Chicago Manual of Style, the Modern Language Association (MLA) and the American Psychological Association (APA). Some industries, professions and even corporations have their own style guide. Choose what's most appropriate to the task.

We recognize that, more and more, people rely on quick online searches to check their grammar, punctuation and word choice. That's certainly better than nothing. We would just caution you to make sure your source is legitimate. Merriam-Webster, Oxford and Macmillan all offer online dictionaries. We also like dictionary.com and thesaurus.com. Grammar Girl (Mignon Fogarty), Grammarly and OWL (University of Purdue's online writing lab) are among the best grammar resources we've seen. There are countless others. Take the time to evaluate them, though, before you rely on them too heavily.

 **I didn't have time to write a short letter so I wrote a long one instead."**

– Mark Twain

## EXERCISE: TAKE A TURN WITH THE AXE

Clear writing is succinct writing. Try rewriting each of the following phrases using fewer, simpler or more precise words.

1. Conduct an investigation
2. Made the statement that
3. At a later date
4. Were found to be in agreement
5. Procure
6. Very, very angry
7. Make use of, utilize
8. Succeed in making
9. Crisis situation
10. On the occasion that
11. Give consideration to
12. The house was actually full
13. Said in a quiet tone of voice
14. Shrugged his shoulders
15. Has the ability to
16. A distance of 35 miles
17. On a daily basis
18. At this point in time

*See suggested fixes on page 107.*

John

Some of the best advice you'll find on writing comes from writing coach Paula LaRocque, whom we mentioned earlier. Do yourself a favor and grab one of her books. We particularly like *The Book on Writing and Championship Writing*.

"Sometimes we slip into gobbledygook when we're trying to soften the message," she says. "Trying to make the message more palatable by manipulating the language sooner or later leads to euphemism, which at best amuses and at worst alienates.

"'That project lost money' becomes 'that project had an adverse impact on anticipated revenue,'" LaRocque says. "We all know by now that 'collateral damage' means killing civilians."[5]

Borrowing from LaRocque, here are three pairs of sentences that demonstrate the difference between unnecessarily wordy writing and the simple, clear kind:

**First Draft:**
Prompted in part by a new anti-smog law that is boosting business' demand for better service, a major reassessment that could lead to big changes in the county's public transportation system is beginning.
**Rewrite:**
Local leaders want to make it easier for county residents to get around without their cars.

**First Draft:**
Should I act upon the urgings that I feel or remain passive and thus cease to exist?
**Rewrite:**
To be or not to be?

**First Draft:**
The biota exhibited a 100 percent mortality response.
**Rewrite:**
The fish died.

# TOP 10 WAYS TO AVOID CREDIBILITY-STEALING GAFFES[6]

We wish we could – but of course we can't – address every potential grammar, style and punctuation question you may have. But we have an idea of what trips people up most often, so we offer these reminders and best practices for your reference. Incorporate these ideas into your writing and you will go a long way toward earning the confidence and respect of your readers. (We opted to repeat a couple must-do's already so you can refer to our top 10 writing tips in one place.)

1. **Know your audience; understand their motivation.**
   Consider what they already know, what they may not know, how they communicate, the vocabulary they use, how much time they will give the topic, and how important it is (or isn't) to them. Write accordingly. In writing, as in verbal communication, knowing your audience should be your top priority.

2. **Use definite, specific language to avoid misunderstanding.**
   Eliminate unnecessary words, flowery language and long explanations. Limit numbers, symbols, jargon, clichés, adjectives, adverbs and inverted sentences. And try not to get enamored with the idioms of the day: expressions like "double down," "unpack," "right?," "circle back" and "socialize" (meaning to share something and let it simmer with a group for a while).

   **Challenge yourself to do these three things when reviewing your work:**

   • Delete words that mean little or nothing (e.g., "as I said").

   • Delete words that repeat the meaning of other words
     (e.g., "introducing a new XYZ").

   • Replace a phrase with a word (e.g., replace "at this point in time"
     with "now" or nothing at all).

**Substitute 'damn' every time you're inclined to write 'very'; your editor will delete it and the writing will be just as it should be."**

– Mark Twain

3. **Be consistent.** Keep to one tense and one voice. Express coordinate ideas in a similar fashion. According to style legends Strunk and White, the unskilled writer often violates the "parallel construction" principle, mistakenly believing in the value of constantly varying the form of expression.[7] (In other words, if you begin a phrase with an "-ing" verb in your first bullet point, begin each of your subsequent bullet-pointed items with an "-ing" verb. It just makes for easier reading.)

4. **Watch your tone.** *Harvard Business Review* publishes an outstanding book, the *HBR Guide to Better Business Writing.* Its author, Bryan Garner, counsels:

Adopt a tone appropriate to your relationship with the recipient. Avoid hyperformality ... Too much formality will spoil your style. Keep your writing down to earth and achieve a personal touch by:

• Writing your message more or less as you'd say it, but without all the "casualisms."

• Including courtesies such as "thank you," "we're happy to" and "we appreciate."

• Using the names of people.

• Using personal pronouns.[8]

5. **Use pronouns correctly.** Too often we see people using "I" as their go-to, regardless of where it falls in the sentence. It's like nails on a chalkboard for many of us and can erode your credibility. Use the pronoun "me," along with other objective pronouns such as us, him, her, you and them, when the pronoun is the object of a verb or preposition. An easy way of making sure you've chosen the right pronoun is to see whether the sentence reads properly if you remove the additional pronouns or nouns in the sentence.

**Here are some examples of correct usage:**

• John and I went for coffee. ("I" is the subject of the verb.)

• The dog followed John and me. ("Me" is the object of the verb.)

• Sue spent the day with Carol and me.
  ("Me" is the object of the preposition.)

Never use "myself" in place of I or me. "Myself" is a reflexive or intensive pronoun. Reflexive: I cut myself. Intensive: I will drive you myself. It is not correct to say, "Address your questions to George and myself." We hear it all the time and it makes us cringe. Don't do that to your readers.

Generally speaking, avoid using too much "I" or ego in your writing. Words like "we" and "our" are warmer and more inclusive. And don't hesitate to use contractions; they make your writing more natural and inviting. If this isn't quite clear (and trust us, we get that this can be confusing), we encourage you to do some further study on your own.

6. **Use active voice.** Change negatives to affirmatives. Rather than focusing on the problem, focus on the solution or action. A positive tone uses fewer words and has been proven to be clearer. By phrasing messages positively, you encourage people to buy into your ideas and build credibility. For instance: Rather than saying, "Don't talk so softly; people can't hear what you're saying," you might say, "Speak up so people can hear your good ideas."

## EMAIL DO'S AND DON'TS

Because email is the most commonly used written communication vehicle in business, we thought it worthwhile to offer some specific do's and don'ts. Here's what's on the top of our list:

1.  Do use a subject line that clearly indicates what the email is about. Avoid the clever and mysterious.

2.  Do get right to the point, politely.

3.  Don't forget your signature, complete with at least two ways to contact you.

4.  Do keep it short.
    Use an attachment or another form of communication if the length exceeds a single screen.

5.  Do be aware that some people (namely, media) will not open attachments. Best to send attachments only to people you know well and with whom you regularly do business.

6.  Nine times out of 10, do use a professional salutation.
    Your grandmother was right: Hey is for horses. That said, it always goes back to knowing your audience.

7.  Do stick to standard capitalization and punctuation. Question use of emojis and emoticons.
    Used well, they can help establish a friendly tone but, generally speaking, they're best to avoid if you don't know the person well.

8.  Do reply to all emails – and within a reasonable time frame.

9.  Don't assume the recipient knows what you're talking about.
    Write your email as a stand-alone message. Avoid a one-word or one-line reply, particularly in external communications.

10. Do copy people judiciously.
    Stop copying them when the conversation shifts and they no longer need to be included.
    Be wary of "reply all." Only copy those who need to know and will understand immediately why they're being copied.

**BONUS:** A March 2018 *Wall Street Journal* roundup on the topic of email gave this good, research-informed advice:

- Don't answer email too quickly or after hours – primarily because these behaviors have proven to be no more or even less efficient and can cause additional stress in the workplace.

- The best time to send email (assuming you want them read) is early in the week and early in the day.

- Don't necessarily listen to conventional wisdom. Goofy spellings and all caps can work well in some situations. And email negotiations also can be successful. It's a matter of taking the time to think through your recipient(s) and responses.[9]

7. **Avoid unnecessary capitalization.** Capitalize proper but not common nouns. Capitalize job titles before names only if the titles are unique to that job. Capitalize departments only when part of a proper noun. Some geographic regions are uppercase. Consult a stylebook when you aren't certain.

8. **Punctuate correctly.**

   - Form the possessive of singular nouns by adding 's, regardless of the final consonant (e.g., Charles's friend, Burns's poems). Exceptions are the possessive of ancient proper names ending in es and is (e.g., Achilles' heel, Isis' temple and Moses' tablet). More often, you would rewrite as the temple of Isis, etc.

   - Never use single quotation marks unless you are quoting words inside another quotation. Yes, you will see single quotes used to offset words; it's wrong. You also will see single quotes used in some newspaper headlines and captions. This is a carry-over from the days of typesetting with limited space. For most of us, we will use single quotations only inside another quotation.

John

- Periods and commas always go inside the quotation marks, except when a parenthetical reference follows.

- Place semicolons outside of quotation marks.

- Place a question mark, exclamation point, dash and colon within closing quotation marks if the punctuation applies to the quotation itself. Place the punctuation outside the closing quotation marks if the punctuation applies to the whole sentence.

- Avoid using exclamation points. They can come off as overly emotional or childish.

- Punctuation goes after parentheses when the parentheses appear within a sentence. When the entire sentence is parenthesized, place the punctuation inside.

- Lowercase the first word following a colon unless it is a proper noun or the start of a complete sentence or question. (Some style experts suggest uppercase is not required unless two or more sentences follow the colon.)

- It is never wrong to include a comma before "and" in a series. It is usually acceptable, however, to omit the serial comma if no confusion arises.


9. **Take time to organize and design your words to facilitate understanding.** In most business writing, you'll put the most important information up front (i.e., your decision or recommendation) and then provide the necessary background. How much you say and in what order will depend largely on your audience and your objective. For additional clarity, consider underlining, bolding, bulleting, numbering or otherwise offsetting information and action required of the recipient. The appearance of your content is important and can facilitate a quicker review and reply. Regardless of the style and formatting guidelines you follow, be consistent but also be prepared to modify to fit a specific situation. Remember, the overriding objective is to be clear.

**Suggested answers from page 99.**
1. Investigate  2. Said  3. Later  4. Agreed  5. Buy  6. Furious  7. Use  8. Made  9. Crisis  10. If  11. Consider  12. The house was full  13. Whispered  14. Shrugged  15. Can  16. 35 miles  17. Daily  18. Now (or nothing)

10. **Use the word you mean.** Examples:

- accept (receive) vs. except (excluding)

- affect (influence, v.) vs. effect (result, n.)

- allude (reference) vs. elude (evade)

- anecdote (story) vs. antidote (medicine)

- anxious (anxiety) vs. eager (look forward to)

- appraise (evaluate) vs. apprise (inform)

- between (2 things) vs. among (3+ things)

- beside (next to) vs. besides (in addition to, apart from)

- backward, not backwards

- chaise longue, not chaise lounge

- champing at the bit, not chomping at the bit

- ensure (to make safe, guarantee) vs. insure (provide insurance)

- farther (go beyond a certain point, literal distance) vs. further (figurative distance as in further thought)

- infer (deduce, conclude) vs. imply (suggest)

- principal (lead person) vs. principle (important, main part of loan or estate, rule)

- stationery (letterhead) vs. stationary (not moving)

- toward, not towards

To write well, read those who write well. Imitate. Practice. If you're uncertain about grammar and style choices, check your stylebook.

We want to end this chapter with some reassuring words from writer William Zinsser:

> "A clear sentence is no accident. Very few sentences come out right the first time, or even the third time. Remember this in moments of despair. If you find that writing is hard, it's because it is hard."[10]

YOUR PRESENCE ON SOCIAL MEDIA
(OR LACK THEREOF)

11

"We do live in this age
of new media."

— S E A L

Social media platforms present opportunities to learn, discover, create, network, build a fan base, promote your company, market products and services, measure success, find work, start a business, engage with family and friends, generate ideas, explore new techniques and simply relax with games, stories and imagery.

They also can be effective tools for enhancing (or detracting from) your public image and reputation.

We won't claim to be social media experts, but we would like to share some thoughts on the topic, as it pertains to mastering executive presence.

## TO POST OR NOT TO POST

In their book *Naked Conversations*, Robert Scoble and Shel Israel make the point that "businesses need to join the conversations because they build trust ... (and) humanize companies, or at least the people who work inside of them ... (and) you can reach thousands, perhaps millions of people for an investment of a few cents and some personal time."[1]

But social media also can be a huge distraction and time-suck.

"Our brains are wired to voraciously feed on information," according to University of California, San Francisco neuroscientist Adam Gazzaley, who co-authored the book *The Distracted Mind*. He says we do ourselves a disservice when we use social media as a break from serious work.

"Our brains need a chance to just be empty," says Gazzaley. He suggests "the best way to help your brain focus is exercise, even for a short period. Just staring into space would be better than refreshing Facebook."[2]

How much you engage in social media – or whether you engage at all – is a personal decision for most people. We say most people because there are positions these days that require active participation in the social stratosphere. Social media can even be a full-time job for some. It's a valuable, often required, work tool for many others.

If you do participate – and you don't want to sabotage the professional reputation you worked so hard to build – we suggest incorporating three best practices. (Note: We said professional. We didn't say stodgy or clichéd or pristine. It's OK, even preferable, to have a personality and stand out.)

**To be yourself in a world that is
constantly trying to make you something
else is the greatest accomplishment."**

– Ralph Waldo Emerson

# BEST PRACTICE #1 BE YOU.

Many social media experts recommend people create their own personal brand. That's fine, as long as it's authentic. We are not proponents of creating a persona in the social space that isn't consistent with who you are in the "real world." (Of course, we're not talking about games that allow you to create alternate identities and universes.)

Forgive us for stating the obvious, but the first thing the vast majority of us do after meeting someone or even coming across an unrecognized name is Google them. Or search for the name on LinkedIn. We don't need your permission. We are going to get an impression of you from that search that will be difficult to erase. You want to make sure it impresses. You don't want the door shut before you even know who has come knocking. So even if you don't actively engage, take the time to search for your name occasionally to ensure you're not being presented in a false or negative way.

# BEST PRACTICE #2 BE TRUTHFUL AND TRANSPARENT.

This goes along with Rule #1, but it's important to make the point that hoaxers and charlatans are not accepted in the social space. No one likes a disingenuous person. But in the social arena, it can be deadly. Comments and opinions travel quickly and often there's no stopping them.

# BEST
# PRACTICE #3 CARE.

Be nice. Don't be too quick. Don't get sloppy. Think about what you're putting out there. It doesn't go away. It doesn't go away. That wasn't a typo; it was worth repeating. Tell your children. Remind your staff.

Beyond that, sure, it's smart to be timely, post original content, demonstrate passion and authority, tell stories, allow for and respond in a timely fashion to comments, link to other sources, avoid corporate speak, be aware of and capitalize on search terms used in your field, and use high-quality visuals and audio. You have to build it well if you want them to come and then come back again.

 **Be kind whenever possible.
It is always possible."**

– Dalai Lama

## THE POWER OF LISTENING

"By now businesses know social media isn't just a broadcast platform," says leading industry blogger Dominique Jackson.[3]

We talked about how important it is to know your audience. We can't think of an easier way to get audience insight than by listening online. Search, follow, friend, join and read posts created by your clients, colleagues, prospects, investors, employees, industry influencers, local community, even competitors. Know your stakeholders and what they're saying and sharing. Whether you opt to comment is your call. But don't underestimate the research capability of social media tools.

"Social listening is the process of tracking conversations around specific topics, keywords, phrases, brands or industries, and leveraging your insights," says Jackson. "If you're only paying attention to notifications, you're missing a huge group of people that are talking about you, your brand and your product."[4]

Beyond that, you can stay current on news, trends, cultural and political shifts, and key issues – and how your audiences are talking about them.

## AH, CHOICES ...

There are so many social platforms out there and they are constantly evolving. We, frankly, don't have a strong point of view on what's good and what's bad, what's here to stay and what's on its way out. The available options continue to grow and shift. We hesitate to mention specific platforms simply because the space changes so quickly. There are some thought leaders suggesting even long-time giants of the space (think Facebook and Twitter) will go away. We'll see.

Don't underestimate the social space, though. It provides a wealth of information and opportunity to those who invest the time to understand it and make it work for them.

## A NOD TO LINKEDIN

We've found LinkedIn to be an exceptionally valuable business tool and do think it will be around awhile. LinkedIn offers opportunities for people to discover each other and network – free of charge. For a fee, you can super-charge that offering and get access to people you would not otherwise have. Many use LinkedIn products to search for full-time employment or part-time and temporary work. LinkedIn also offers worthwhile video lectures in its learning center at https://www.linkedin.com/learning/me?trk=nav_neptune_learning.

## LET'S TALK BLOGOSPHERE

Blogging (or vlogging – the video-based version of blogging) is a great way to raise your profile and convey your point of view. It can, no doubt, be part of an effective positioning strategy for executives. Let's consider podcasting, too, in this discussion.

The bottom line: To deliver the results you want, you have to do it right. And no matter what some people may tell you, that takes time and work. It's not OK to wing it or have someone else post for you.

In the words of Chris Brogan, CEO of Owner Media Group and well-respected blogger and social media author, it's time to "stop the bullshit."

Brogan can be a little irreverent but we generally like what he has to say. This is from a recent blog post:

> "We have to stop phoning it in. Everyone. You. Me. Those guys. It's not okay. It's boring and it's messing up the entire opportunity to reach people and help them succeed ...
>
> People will hate us if we're ... just clogging up someone's attention with junk, reruns, leftovers, and generic clones ... Sameness kills ... We need to earn the right to sell and serve, not throw junk over the wall. We just have to do better ... Help people. Equip them for success. It's the best way to market. Treat them like they are in the right place and among like-minded souls. That's the work."[5]

**If blogging is something you're considering, we recommend you do the following:**

- **Post regularly** (at least once per week) and follow our three social media rules above; that is: be yourself, be authentic, and approach with care.

- **Be provocative. Be interesting. Be thoughtful.**

- **Stay on message; consistency is important in building credibility.** (That said, there's something to be said for the occasional unexpected twist or surprise. But do use good judgment. Know your audience. The last thing you want to be is a bore.)

- **Be sure all posts are proofed by someone with writing/grammar/ punctuation expertise.**

- **Have fun with it (or no one else will).** If your business/topic is serious, obviously respect that. But try not to take yourself too seriously. You'll quickly lose your following.

- **Write short.** No one has the patience or time for long rants. Brogan suggests 300-500 words is a good length for a blog post but acknowledge some stats suggest you can go a bit longer.[6]

## A WORD ON FORUMS

There are countless ways to engage online in industry and subject-area forums or "chat rooms." Even Facebook, thought by many to be purely social, offers myriad professional groups. Many find these groups extraordinarily valuable for expert-positioning and networking. As with all social media, however, take appropriate care.

And don't be strictly a taker. Don't use the group as a forum for chest-beating. You must add value. You must take your turn at being a giver. You may ask for a referral or opinions about a service. You may ask other professionals to share intellectual property. That's all fair – as long as you pay it back and forward. It's a give-and-take proposition.

## LEADING THROUGH SOCIAL?

Social media analyst and best-selling author Charlene Li acknowledged in an *Inc.* interview that being active on social media is different for leaders. "It's one thing for your organization to be tweeting and making videos and sharing content, and it's quite a different thing for you as a leader to go out there."[7]

Many top executives feel, legitimately, they don't have the time. Others prefer to be more private. Some just don't see the point.

Li's interviewer, Tom Foster, contends, "Leadership is an art and everyone does it differently; a single blueprint for how to do it right doesn't exist." But Foster also makes the case that social media is "a powerful tool that can't be ignored," enabling leaders to "understand customers' and employees' interests and concerns in large numbers, all at once."

Li concurs, but says it's really an individual choice. "I just want (leaders) to have looked at it and decided some other (approach) is better for them. Otherwise, they could be missing out on a huge competitive advantage."

Leaders can "become facilitators who accelerate the spread of information and shape the decision-making process," Li says. "(They) can personally engage with individuals or groups through multiple touch points, thereby cultivating and transforming relationships purposefully."[8]

## BE THE PURPLE COW

Social media rock star Seth Godin makes the point that purple cows are remarkable; brown cows are not. One is the center of attention; the other is boring. He bases his book, *Purple Cow*, on two concepts:

**1**
**Ideas that spread win.**
**Find something worthwhile to talk about.**

**2**
**Remarkability is in the eye of the consumer.**
**It doesn't matter how hard you worked on something or how important it is to you. It has to matter to your intended receiver.**[9]

We'll leave it there.

## 12

## UNDER PRESSURE

"If you want to
change the world,
be your very best in the
darkest moments ...
(and) don't back down
from the sharks."

—ADMIRAL WILLIAM H. MCRAVEN,
RETIRED NAVY SEAL
AND AUTHOR OF MAKE YOUR BED

John

In this chapter, we discuss how to exude confidence and communicate effectively in fast-breaking, sensitive, "high-stakes" or otherwise challenging situations. Remaining calm and being effective in challenging times are hallmarks of someone who has achieved a high level of executive presence.

We were careful not to use the term "crisis communications" in the title of this chapter because we want to go a bit wider than that. There are myriad situations in our business lives that wouldn't be classified as true crises, but that do call for more thoughtful and prudent handling.

We also didn't want to make this exclusively a "working with the media" chapter because when you have a delicate situation, you have a great many more audiences to consider.

Regardless of the situations you confront, maintaining a confident calm is job one. This will assure others that they can trust and follow your lead. Your poise under pressure also will likely have a positive domino effect, keeping everyone around you from panicking.

## HOW TO PLAN AND PREPARE FOR THE UNEXPECTED

The key to handling a crisis or delicate matter effectively is advance preparation. While you often can't predict what might happen or when something might occur, you can do a number of things in advance to ensure you're prepared when the unexpected or unpleasant arrives at your door. Most companies have, and regularly update and review, operational plans, safety protocols and crisis communications plans. If your organization does not have formal processes in place, it likely has informal ones. Being familiar with and practicing these protocols, of course, is extremely important.

**Following are some best practices in crisis planning and preparedness:**

- Establish a crisis/response team and identify clear roles and backups. It's especially important to know who's in charge and who has to sign off on what.

- Do everything in your power to mitigate risk. Conduct an annual assessment of risk with the help of risk management and crisis communications experts; address vulnerabilities.

- Identify most likely crisis scenarios in your company/industry and play them out. Create detailed action plans for each one.

- Build and regularly update a comprehensive media list. Get to know your local media, as well as the journalists who regularly cover your industry and issues.

- Identify all other constituents and regularly update contact information. Know who you need to reach and how you will reach them in the event of a crisis. Don't forget public officials, community and business leaders, retirees, volunteers, industry associations, law enforcement, first responders and regulatory agencies.

- Develop core messages that can serve as a starting point when crafting your response to a prickly situation.

- Craft a draft standby statement and standby webpage that can be used while you gather your facts and prepare a more detailed response.

- Prepare fact sheets, news release templates, media consent forms, maps, biographies, information sharing policies, social media policies, photographs, video footage and other appropriate documents that may be needed.

- Put together a list of key professional consultants you may require, such as legal, financial, insurance and risk management, public relations, investor relations, government relations and advertising counsel. Also be sure you can easily access vendors (photographers, videographers, printers, wire service, media monitoring service, sign makers, etc.).

- Consider arranging for an off-site crisis command center, call-in service and emergency kits.

- Conduct at least annual crisis simulations to test your response effectiveness.

Being prepared to address a challenge quickly is key to maintaining trust in any high-stakes, fast-moving situation.

## HOW TO COMMUNICATE IN A CRISIS OR HIGH-STAKES SITUATION

**Doing the best at this moment puts you in the best place for the next moment."**

– Oprah Winfrey

Most important in communicating in a crisis is providing clear, accurate and immediate information – recognizing there frequently are legal, ethical, safety and humane considerations to be weighed.

While attorneys often favor saying nothing or as little as possible, the court of public opinion says otherwise. "Tell it all and tell it fast" is the mantra you'll hear in the halls of most crisis communications and public relations firms. When information is shared, emotions and rumors subside.

There is no option to wait in our "real-time" world. The word will get out and it will get out fast. It's best to get out there ahead of others and help frame the story in the media and among your key constituents. In the media's telling of a crisis, you will see that a victim, a villain and a hero generally emerge. You don't want to be pegged the villain or even the victim. Act as a hero would act.

Additionally, attempt to reach all audiences at the same time. Do not let priority constituents (employees, shareholders, customers, board members) learn about the incident only through the media, other mass communication or the rumor mill.

More than one communication will likely be needed with each audience segment. Plan on an ongoing dialogue until the crisis is over, and then be sure to follow up when things have died down, as well. Crises can test you. But they can be managed and even lead to relationship-strengthening and brand-building opportunities.

## HOW TO DELIVER BAD OR DIFFICULT NEWS

Your objective in delivering bad or difficult news is to deliver it clearly, succinctly and with compassion. You want your message heard and understood. We recommend you organize your message as follows:

- **State the news** or key message upfront. What went wrong?
  Deliver the information firmly, factually, yet with appropriate concern.

- **Explain why** it happened and how you're fixing it.
  Commit to identifying and addressing the root causes of the problem.

- **Empathize.** Acknowledge how difficult the news is for the person/people hearing it. Express your concern and support. Also indicate how it impacts the organization, its stakeholders and the broader community.

- **Express confidence** that the situation will be resolved and the company will remain true to its vision, mission and core values.

- **Describe next steps** and any specific help/resources they will be provided to get through the situation.

- **Answer questions.** Address them as fully as possible.
  (See Q&A section later in this chapter.)

- **Follow up.** Consider using any and all forms of communication that are
  appropriate to the situation and available to you (e.g., verbal, email,
  formal written letter, newsletter, video, telephone, text, web-based content,
  social media, advertising).

- **Be consistent** in all messaging.

## ENGAGING WITH THE MEDIA

While the traditional news media still plays a big role in a major crisis, the media
landscape has become much larger and much more nuanced.

When working with the media, remember that they, like you, are simply people
with a job to do. They are under pressure to get the story first, but also to get it
right. If you take the time to establish a relationship with them before disaster
strikes – or at least know who they are, understand what they care about, and
respect their deadlines and preferences – you'll be much more successful when
the stakes are high. Try to be helpful. If you can't answer a question, tell them
why. If you can't provide missing information immediately, tell them when you
will be in a position to get that to them. A spirit of cooperation, respect and
courtesy goes a long, long way.

**When in a conversation with the media, executive presence means you establish yourself as a credible, reliable source and ...**

| ALWAYS | NEVER |
|---|---|
| Defer to the designated spokesperson if you're not the most authoritative source. | Never feel obligated to respond to media inquiries if it's not your role/place. Direct them to the appropriate spokesperson. |
| Prepare and organize your talking points in advance to the extent possible. | Never wing it. |
| Stick to known facts. It's OK to say you don't know. | Never speculate or offer opinions. |
| Talk in short sound bites. You'll be better understood and minimize your risk of being edited. | Never be long-winded. |
| Assume it will appear in print/on air if you say it. | Never go off the record. |
| Be conversational, accommodating and as positive as appropriate under the situation. | Never appear defensive, agitated or angry. Don't patronize or talk over the reporter's head. Avoid using technical jargon if it can be helped. |
| Explain why you cannot offer the information now (but when you might). Get back to the reporter in as timely a matter as possible – even if you weren't successful in securing information. | Never say "no comment." Never guess. Never lie. |
| Talk about your company and the industry in general. | Never speak negatively (or at all) about competitors. |
| Explain that certain, more serious issues require careful investigation. Leaders earn respect when they are willing to publicly take their lumps. | Never cast blame or admit liability without first fully vetting with appropriate consultants and experts on your team. |

## THE Q&A

A question-and-answer session is a wonderful way to continue a friendly dialogue after a formal presentation. It's an opportunity for the audience to increase their understanding, share their own thoughts and experiences, and dive deeper into a topic of interest.

In a crisis or contentious situation, the Q&A can look a lot different. We are going to focus on the crisis Q&A, but many of the principles can be applied to any Q&A discussion.

**Here's what we coach:**

• Prepare ahead of time. Develop a list of questions you know will be asked. Include those ugly, contentious questions you hope you won't get. Develop responses for every question and include "bridges" that can help you get from "ugly" back to your key messages.

• Listen to the whole question and then repeat it. This buys you a bit of time and ensures everyone in the room heard the question. In many instances, you'll want to take the opportunity to rephrase the question. In your paraphrasing, try to take the emotion out of the question. Make it more clear, positive and relevant. Take care not to "spin" the question; you want to stay true to the issue being raised and answer what's being asked. This does take practice.

• Answer the question directly, and then explain further as necessary. If your response gets long, be sure to tie your final remarks back to the original question.

• Once you answer the question, put the shovel down and stop talking! As speakers we sometimes think more is better. Wrong. Short is better – if it answers the question. The audience will ask for more should they need/want it.

## 15 GAME-CHANGING TIPS FROM A SEASONED MEDIA PRO

Our friend and colleague Tom Chizmadia is senior vice president of government affairs and communications at Lehigh Hanson, Inc., one of the largest construction materials companies in North America. Having served for decades in the roles of corporate spokesperson and media trainer, he had some cogent advice and insights to share:

1. Know who you're talking to. "Know the reporter and understand his/her depth of knowledge and understanding of the topic. Don't hesitate to ask questions of a reporter." (By the way, have you ever been to a plant? Do you know how cement is made? Are you familiar with our industry's regulatory issues?)

2. Understand who will be seeing your comments in the press. "This tells you what level of detail you need to get into."

3. Know your subject matter. "Really look into the issue ahead of time. Think through the 'what if' questions."

4. Practice ahead of time. "Pick up your phone and record yourself responding to posed questions, or call a colleague and practice your responses."

5. Address reporter (questioner) by name.

6. Look at the reporter, not the camera. "The reporter will react; the camera won't."

7. Take a big breath and speak slowly. "This will help the audience understand you better. But it also will help relax you and give you confidence."

8. Connect with the audience. "Be real. I'm a big believer in eye contact and body movement."

9. Talk in sound bites. Do not talk long, but do not give one- or two-word answers either.

10. Be yourself. "It helps to have a personality. Be professional, not robotic. Show appropriate emotion."

11. Don't play favorites. "Address every question with the same importance. Don't evaluate questions."

12. When rephrasing a question, get to the heart of the issue. What is the reporter really asking? "They may ask what at first sounds like a confrontational question about emission levels when they really just want to know if the community is safe."

13. You have good reasons for not wanting to answer some questions; share them. "I often will say, 'Look, I appreciate your wanting to know X, but corporate policy is X' or 'Please understand we are not legally permitted to comment on X' or 'My competitors would love to get that information, but I'm not going to be the one to give it to them ...'"

14. Don't speak nonstop. Engage.

15. Remember: Everyone has a phone and everyone is a citizen journalist. Expect anything you say to be shared broadly.

> **In every (moment of) crisis, doubt or confusion, take the higher path – the path of compassion, courage, understanding and love."**
>
> – Amit Ray, in *Nonviolence: The Transforming Power*

# REFLECTION: WHERE ARE YOU MOST VULNERABLE?

Many crises could have been avoided, if only ...

Take time to conduct a risk assessment of the space you occupy, if only informally. What action(s) can you take now to lower your risk of disaster? How can you make your environment safer, more compliant, more inclusive, more diverse, more environmentally friendly, less tolerant of harassment, more accountable, more communicative? What should stop?

Commit to actions you will take to improve the situation.

# CONCLUSION

"The single biggest
problem in
communication
is the illusion that it has
taken place."

– GEORGE BERNARD SHAW

**What we have here is a failure to communicate *well*.**

The number one skill gap in America's workforce is communication, according to a 2018 Workforce Report published by LinkedIn.[1] Stop and think about that for a minute. How can this be? It's dumbfounding.

In its coverage of these findings, CNBC also reported the job platform Monster found that the ability to communicate effectively is one of the most in-demand "soft skills." This was based on its analysis of some 940,000 job listings. CNBC's segment also cited a 2016 study published in the *Journal of Education*, which found managers pay special attention to communication skills when evaluating an employee.[2]

On the positive side, we're seeing an uptick in investment in communications, presentation skills, media and leadership training. Leaders are recognizing the critical role communication skills will have on the future performance of their organizations as the workplace continues to evolve into a collaborative, human-and-machine environment.

As technology continues to infiltrate how we work, our human interaction skills need to be upgraded, says Cheryl Cran, future-of-work consultant and author of *The Art of Change Leadership.* "Master communicators have solid listening skills, the ability to tune into a person with focus, and the ability to articulate clearly."[3] **They have executive presence.**

A Deloitte study of 2018 tech trends definitively places oral and written expression and comprehension, speech clarity, critical thinking, emotional intelligence, persuasion, reason, negotiation and active listening skills on the human end of the spectrum.[4] We'll need people with these skills more than ever as the "no-collar" workforce gains ground.

We have been further encouraged to see communications and presentation skills training incorporated into more academic programs at colleges and universities across the country. Communications has expanded beyond the confines of journalism, mass communications and interpersonal communications departments. Because, yes, we need to effectively communicate in business, mathematics, science, medicine, sports, entertainment, art and any other academic, career or life pursuit one might imagine.

We were enormously pleased when John Keyser agreed to write the foreword to this book. John has been coaching leaders for decades and always has espoused the importance of communication and executive presence. In his recently released book, *When Leadership Improves, Everyone Wins*, he makes a great point; he says, "One giant step we can all take is to become a better listener ... To truly understand another person, listening is critically important ... It takes conscious practice." When we listen, Johns says, and "when we lead with integrity, humility, and a commitment to serve ... we will stand apart."[5] Indeed.

We hope you benefited in some tangible way from reading our book. We hope, at minimum, you made a commitment to yourself to improve your communications effectiveness through practice.

Communicating effectively and mastering executive presence are career-changing, life-enhancing pursuits. They do require your time and energy. But, we promise you, they are well worth that time and energy.

 **There is no passion to be found playing small – in settling for a life that is less than the one you are capable of living."**
– Nelson Mandela

We wish you much success and enjoyment in your
future learning and work.

# ENDNOTES

## PREFACE

i Janelle Weaver, "Social before Birth: Twins First Interact with Each Other as Fetuses; Twins Interact Purposefully in the Womb," *Scientific American.* January 1, 2011. https://www.scientificamerican.com/article/social-before-birth/.

ii John M. Vautier and John J. Vautier, *Speak As Well As You Think: An Executive's Guide to Excellence in Public Speaking* (Michigan, Nostina Novi, 2013).

## CHAPTER ONE

1 I'm reasonably certain my college friend didn't create the idiom, but I've never been able to determine the source. Please forgive the lack of proper attribution.

2 John Beeson, "Deconstructing Executive Presence," *Harvard Business Review*, August 22, 2012. https://hbr.org/2012/08/de-constructing-executive-pres.

3 Sylvia Ann Hewlett, *Executive Presence: The Missing Link between Merit and Success* (New York: Harper Collins Publishers, 2014), 1.

4 Ibid., 16.

5 Ibid., 16-41.

6 Beeson.

7 Hewlett, 37-42.

[8] August Turak, "Are You Coachable? The Five Steps to Coachability," *Forbes*. September 30, 2011. https://www.forbes.com/sites/augustturak/2011/09/30/are-you-coachable-the-five-steps-to-coachability/#312fd08724f6.

[9] Malcolm Gladwell, *Outliers: The Story of Success* (New York: Little, Brown and Company, 2008), 40-41.

## CHAPTER TWO

[1] Daniela Schiller, Jonathan B. Freeman, Jason P. Mitchell, James S. Uleman and Elizabeth A. Phelps, "A Neural Mechanism of First Impressions," *Nature Neuroscience* 12, no. 4 (2009): 508-514.

[2] Rick Nauert Ph.D., "Why First Impressions Are Difficult to Change: Study," *Livescience*. January 19, 2011. https://www.livescience.com/10429-impressions-difficult-change-study.html.

[3] Malcolm Gladwell, *Blink: The Power of Thinking without Thinking* (New York: Little, Brown and Company, 2005), 18-47.

[4] Ibid., 44.

[5] Heidi Grant, "A Second Chance to Make the Right Impression," *Harvard Business Review*. January-February 2015 issue. https://hbr.org/2015/01/a-second-chance-to-make-the-right-impression.

[6] Ibid.

[7] Chris Anderson, *TED Talks: The Official TED Guide to Public Speaking* (New York: First Mariner Books, 2017), 180.

[8] Ibid., 179-182.

[9] Peggy Noonan, *What I Saw at the Revolution* (New York: Random House, Inc., 1990), 4.

[10] Amy Cuddy, *Presence* (New York: Little, Brown and Company, 2015), 19-20.

[11] Ibid., 24-25.

[12] Ibid., 25.

## CHAPTER THREE

[1] Nancy Duarte, *HBR Guide to Persuasive Presentations* (Boston: Harvard Business Review Press, 2012), 17.

[2] Ibid.

[3] Jodi Harris, "Quick and Dirty Guide for Creating Actionable Content Marketing Personas," Content Marketing Institute. September 10, 2017. https://contentmarketinginstitute.com/2017/09/actionable-content-marketing-personas/.

4 Ibid.

## CHAPTER FOUR

[1] Cuddy, 5.

[2] Ibid, 21.

[3] James Wood, "Muscle-Bound: Tom Wolfe's 'Back to Blood,'" *The New Yorker*. October 15, 2012. https://www.newyorker.com/magazine/2012/10/15/muscle-bound.

[4] A nod to the legendary Meat Loaf, Jim Steinman and their "Paradise by the Dashboard Light."

[5] Duarte, 12.

## CHAPTER FIVE

[1] Anderson, 30, 36.

[2] Ibid., 35-37.

## CHAPTER SIX

[1] Rob Capps, "First Impressions: The Science of Meeting People," WIRED.com. November 20, 2012. https://www.wired.com/2012/11/amy-cuddy-first-impressions/.

[2] Cuddy, 226.

[3] Ibid., 223.

[4] Ibid.

[5] Ron Gutman, "The Hidden Power of Smiling," TED2011. https://www.ted.com/talks/ron_gutman_the_hidden_power_of_smiling/transcript?language=en.

## CHAPTER SEVEN

[1] Bronwyn Fryer, "Storytelling That Moves People," *Harvard Business Review.* June 2003. https://hbr.org/2003/06/storytelling-that-moves-people.

[2] Ibid.

[3] Anderson, 65.

[4] Eric Ransdell, "The Nike Story? Just Tell It!" *Fast Company.* December 31, 1999.

[5] Ibid.

[6] Daniel Coyle, *The Little Book of Talent* (New York: Random House, 2012), 5.

[7] Fryer.

[8] Ibid.

[9] Annette Simmons, *The Story Factor* (New York: Basic Books, 2001), 199-218.

## CHAPTER EIGHT

[1] Scott Berinato, *Good Charts: The HBR Guide to Making Smarter, More Persuasive Data Visualizations* (Boston: Harvard Review Press, 2016), 111-112.

[2] Ibid., 184.

## CHAPTER NINE

[1] David Kelley and Tom Kelley, *Creative Confidence: Unleashing the Creative Potential within Us All* (New York: Crown Business, 2013), 64-65.

[2] Marshall Goldsmith, *Triggers* (New York: Crown Publishing Group, 2015), 173-174.

[3] Coyle, 97-98.

[4] Ibid., 100-101.

[5] Ibid., 77-80.

## CHAPTER TEN

[1] Joseph M. Williams and Gregory G. Colomb, Style: *Lessons in Clarity and Grace* (Boston: Longman, 2010), 160.

[2] Paula LaRocque, *The Book on Writing: The Ultimate Guide to Writing Well* (Arlington, Texas: Grey and Guvnor, 2003), 6-7.

[3] Williams and Colomb, 193.

[4] Ibid.

[5] LaRocque, 27.

[6] Sources: APA (American Psychological Association) Style Manual, Associated Press Stylebook, Strunk and White's *The Elements of Style,* Paula LaRocque's *The Book on Writing* Chapter 25: Style Guide.

[7] William Strunk, Jr. and E. B. White, *The Elements of Style* (Essex, UK: Pearson, 2013), 25.

[8] Bryan A. Garner, *HBR Guide to Better Business Writing* (Boston: Harvard Business Review Press, 2012), 99-100.

[9] Andrew Blackman, "The Smartest Ways to Use Email at Work," *The Wall Street Journal.* March 11, 2018. https://www.wsj.com/articles/the-smartest-ways-to-use-email-at-work-1520820300.

[10] William Zinsser, *On Writing Well: The Classic Guide to Writing Nonfiction* (New York: Harper Perennial, 2016), 9.

## CHAPTER ELEVEN

[1] Robert Scoble and Shel Israel, *Naked Conversations: How Blogs Are Changing the Way Businesses Talk with Customers* (Hoboken, N.J.: John Wiley & Sons, Inc., 2006), 27.

[2] Geoffrey A. Fowler, "Take Back Your Brain from Social Media," *The Wall Street Journal.* February 1, 2017. https://www.wsj.com/articles/take-back-your-brain-from-social-media-1485968678.

[3] Dominique Jackson, "What Is Social Listening & Why Is It Important?" Sprout Social (sproutsocial.com). September 20, 2017. https://sproutsocial.com/insights/social-listening/.

[4] Ibid.

[5] Chris Brogan, "Quit Your Bullshit," chrisbrogan.com. March 10, 2018. https://chrisbrogan.com/quit-bullshit/.

[6] Brogan, "What I Told the Bloggers at Social Media Marketing World," chrisbrogan.com. March 23, 2017. https://chrisbrogan.com/smmw17/.

[7] Tom Foster, "Charlene Li Touts the Benefits of Social Media for Top Leaders," *Inc.* March 18, 2015. https://www.inc.com/tom-foster/charlene-li-the-three-keys-to-harnessing-social-media-for-leadership.html.

[8] Ibid.

[9] Seth Godin, Purple Cow: Transform Your Business by Being Remarkable (New York: Portfolio, 2009), 40.

## CONCLUSION

[1] Ruth Umoh, "The CEO of LinkedIn Shares the No. 1 Job Skill American Employees Are Lacking," CNBC.com. April 26, 2018. https://www.cnbc.com/2018/04/26/linkedin-ceo-the-no-1-job-skill-american-employees-lack.html.

[2] Ibid.

[3] Catherine Clifford, "6 Ways Work Is Changing and 6 Skills That Will Help You Succeed," CNBC.com. March 29, 2017. https://www.cnbc.com/2017/03/29/6-ways-work-is-changing-and-6-skills-that-will-help-you-succeed.html.

[4] Anthony Abbatiello, Tim Boehm, Jeff Schwartz and Sharon Chand, "No-Collar Workforce: Humans and Machines in One Loop – Collaborating in Roles and New Talent Models: Tech Trends 2018," *Deloitte Insights.* December 5, 2017. https://www2.deloitte.com/insights/us/en/focus/tech-trends/2018/no-collar-workforce.html.

[5] John Keyser, *When Leadership Improves, Everyone Wins: A Discussion of the Principles of Highly Effective Leadership* (Book Baby, 2018), 21-23.

## SUGGESTED READING

Anderson, Chris.
*TED Talks: The Official TED Guide to Public Speaking* (2016) 269 pages

Berinato, Scott.
*Good Charts: The HBR Guide to Making Smarter, More Persuasive Data Visualizations* (2016) 255 pages

Coyle, Daniel.
*The Little Book of Talent: 52 Tips for Improving Your Skills* (2012) 160 pages

Cuddy, Amy.
*Presence: Bringing Your Boldest Self to Your Biggest Challenges* (2015) 344 pages

Duarte, Nancy.
*HBR Guide to Persuasive Presentations: Inspire Action, Engage the Audience, Sell Your Ideas* (2012) 229 pages

Duarte, Nancy.
*Resonate: Present Visual Stories That Transform Audiences* (2010) 272 pages

Duckworth, Angela.
*Grit: The Power of Passion and Perseverance* (2016) 333 pages

Gallo, Carmine.
*Talk Like TED: The 9 Public Speaking Secrets of the World's Top Minds* (2015). 278 pages

Garner, Bryan A.
*HBR Guide to Better Business Writing: Engage Readers, Tighten and Brighten, Make Your Case* (2012) 210 pages

Gladwell, Malcolm.
*Outliers: The Story of Success* (2011) 336 pages

Hewlett, Sylvia Ann.
*Executive Presence: The Missing Link between Merit and Success* (2014) 210 pages

Kelley, Tom and David Kelley.
*Creative Confidence: Unleashing the Creative Potential within Us All* (2013) 278 pages

McRaven, Admiral William H.
*Make Your Bed: The Little Things That Can Change Your Life .... And Maybe the World* (2017) 130 pages

Noonan, Peggy.
*The Time of Our Lives: Collected Writings* (2015) 445 pages

Reynolds, Garr.
*Presentation Zen: Simple Ideas on Presentation Design and Delivery* (2nd Edition) (2011) 312 pages

Strunk, William, Jr.
*The Elements of Style* (2017) 96 pages

Williams, Joseph M. and Joseph Bizup.
*Style: Lessons in Clarity and Grace* (2016) 256 pages

Zinsser, William.
*On Writing Well: The Classic Guide to Writing Nonfiction* (2016) 321 pages

## ABOUT THE AUTHORS

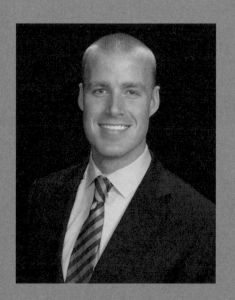